150 Tips and Tricks for the Kindle Fire and Kindle Fire HD

Summary

This report is dedicated to looking at all sorts of tips and tricks that can be used on the Amazon Kindle Fire and Kindle Fire HD. These two digital readers can be used with several controls relating to how books are read, how people can go online and how their data can be protected. This report is arranged into several easy to use chapters to show you everything you can do with your reader.

Everything in this guide is even divided to show you what you can use for individual activities. You can learn about how to play music files, convert files into formats that the Kindle Fire can use and even learn how to get third party applications onto the Kindle Fire. This is all arranged with a series of pictures of what you can do and a number of steps for each individual tip or trick. Be sure to refer to this guide often when taking a look at what you can do with your Kindle Fire.

Contents

Chapter 1 – Introduction

Are you aware of what your Amazon Kindle Fire or Kindle Fire HD can do for you? It's one of the best devices you can use for reading things but you have to be sure that you know what you can do with it before you actually try it out.

This guide is all about teaching you how to use the Kindle Fire or Kindle Fire HD to do all sorts of fun things. These include some things that you might never have imagined you could do with such a device. You can learn how to master the control on the Kindle Fire or know how to use all the best features of the device when reading a book. You can also learn about how to use the many media playback features that it has to offer.

This guide also lists information on how you can use the Kindle Fire to do all sorts of fun things online. The things you can do with your Wi-Fi connection are impressive and have to be seen so you can enjoy the most out of your reader.

You can also learn about several topics relating to taking care of some of the problems that often come with the use of the Kindle Fire. It's true that this is a useful device but there are times when it might no work as well as it should. You can learn in this guide how to fix many problems relating to both the software you are trying to use and the physical properties that come with the reader.

It's especially important to think about the ways how you can protect your device by keeping your kids under control when using it. You can use a few special tips and tricks with regards to parental controls in mind. These are made to help you control your reader so kids will not be likely to get into the wrong spots.

You might be amazed at the things that you can do with the Kindle Fire or Kindle Fire HD. This guide will show you 150 of the different things that you can get out of this unique device. The many things that you can do with the Amazon Kindle Fire are unique and show just how impressive this product truly is for all your entertainment needs.

8

[illegible]

[illegible]

[illegible]

[illegible]

[illegible]

[illegible]

Chapter 2 – Using the Keyboard

The keyboard is an important part of the Kindle Fire and Kindle Fire HD. This digital display will allow you to enter in information on the Kindle as needed so you can add notes to your books, enter in website addresses and even send emails. There are several things that you can do with your keyboard to make it a little more useful for whatever you'd like to make out of it.

Be aware of the ?123 button located on the bottom left of the keyboard because it will be used on a number of occasions in this section. Don't forget to notice the smaller characters in the individual keys.

1. Double Space Period

The double space period function is made to let you end sentences and move to new ones as needed. Here's how you can do this.

1. Hold your finger down on the period sign.
2. Move the finger with a swipe to the space bar.
3. Release the space bar after you do this. You should now have a period and a space added to the end of a sentence.

2. Cut/Copy and Paste Items

Here's how you can cut or copy and paste items with the keyboard.

1. Highlight the part of the text that you want to cut or copy.
2. Swipe your keyboard from the ?123 key to the c key if you want to copy the text or to the x key if you want to cut it.
3. Open a new program that you want to enter your text into. This can include a notepad or even an email drafting program.
4. Swipe the keyboard from the ?123 key to the v key to paste the item you highlighted into the new window.

This is practically the same as what you might do when you are using a traditional computer keyboard. The only difference is that you will hold your finger down on the keyboard while using the ?123 button as the main button.

The Swype feature on the Kindle Fire keyboard is the key part of what can be used to make it easier for you to change all of these features. This is all used to improve your keyboard's ability to quickly enter in data without having to switch from one part of the screen to the next.

3. Add www.

Are you tired of having to add the same www. addition to every single website you enter in? This can be problematic if you want to use the Kindle Fire to access the desktop version of a site instead of the mobile version (we will talk a little more about that later on in this book). Here's a simple process used to help out with entering in this www. addition as quickly as possible.

1. Hold onto the w key.
2. Swipe your finger to the period key.
3. The www. entry should be added to the domain name you are trying to enter in.

4. Turn Off Auto Correction

The Auto Correction feature on the Kindle Fire keyboard sounds like a good idea in practice. It makes it easier for the Kindle Fire to fix your mistakes while you are writing them. However, sometimes it can cause embarrassing typos that might look awkward. This is especially difficult to deal with if you are not completely sure of how to spell a certain word.

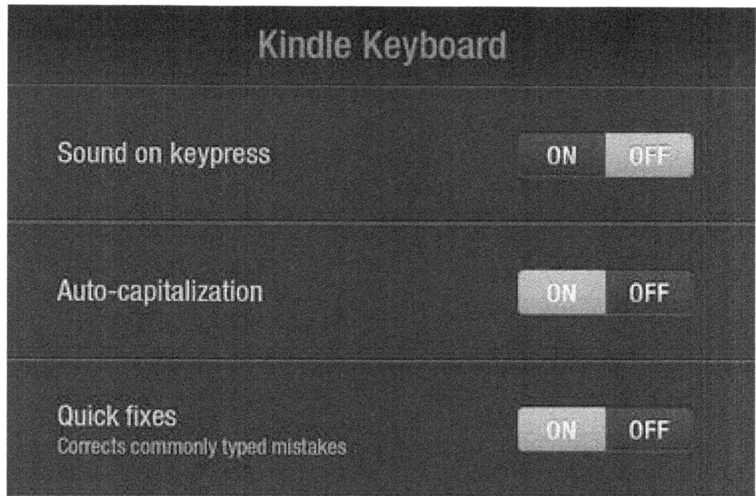

You can turn off this Auto Correction feature with these simple steps:

1. Press and hold onto the space bar.
2. Tap the Keyboard Settings opening.
3. Turn the Quick Fixes option off. This is the part of the keyboard used to correct common typos in your work. This may also be used to turn off to Auto Correction feature.

Remember, you can turn this feature off but you can't turn off the feature that predicts what you will be typing next. Still, you can choose to not use the predictive feature on the Kindle Fire if you do not have a need for it.

5. Change the Keyboard's Language

The Kindle Fire can use a number of different international keyboard settings. This can be useful if you are looking to enter in something with a different language and need to use a specialized keyboard that uses different symbols based on the language you are using.

1. Install the GO Launcher EX application onto your Kindle Fire. This should be free to use.
2. Install the AnyCut program to reveal the functions hidden within your Kindle Fire. You will have to use the Go Launcher EX application to complete the action instead of the standard Kindle launcher.
3. Go to the New Shortcut section of the AnyCut program and then choose Activity.
4. Select the Input Languages menu to bring up a full listing of the different keyboard layouts that you can add to the Kindle.

This should allow you to select the appropriate keyboard for whatever language you want to use. As you can see, you can use not only languages with Latin characters but also languages with some specific character designs. These include the Russian language as noticed on the top of this example.

6. How to Turn the Sound On When Pressing Keys

Sometimes it helps to keep the sound on when pressing keys on the keyboard. This is so you will know that you are actually entering in things as needed. Here's a look at how you can turn the sound on.

1. Press and hold the space bar to bring up the keyboard menu that we mentioned earlier.
2. Tap the Sound on Keypress option to the On switch.
3. The keypad should now make a sound as you type on it.

This may be used if you want to make your keyboard easier to use. You can always control the volume to adjust how loud the keyboard will be as you enter things into it. This may help you out considering that a vibration feature may not be included when entering things into a keyboard.

7. Quick Number Access

You can quickly enter in numbers without having to keep on switching from the letter arrangement on the keyboard to the number arrangement.

1. Place your finger on the ?123 button.
2. Move the finger with a swipe to the appropriate key that features a number as a secondary entry.
3. This process can be repeated when adding other special characters onto your documents.

8. The Hidden Caps Lock

The caps lock feature on the Kindle Fire or Kindle Fire HD can be accessible even though the keyboard does not specifically has a caps lock button on it.

1. Double-tap the Shift key. This should be the key that has an upward-pointing arrow on it.
2. The Kindle Fire will now type in nothing but capital letters.
3. Double-tap the Shift key again to turn the caps lock feature off.

This should be used regardless of the type of specific keyboard you use on the Kindle Fire. This includes different keyboards that are used for different languages.

9. Capitalize the First Letter

You can quickly capitalize the first letter of a word without having to switch from one spot on the keyboard to the next. Here's a quick look at how you can capitalize the first letter of a word without having to use more keystrokes than needed.

1. Touch the first letter of the word you want to enter. Do not lift your finger off of the keyboard.
2. Swipe upward off of the keyboard without moving the finger off.
3. Swipe over to the second letter in the word.
4. The first letter should be capitalized while the second is in a lower case form. This should be used at any point in your sentence. Of course, the first letter of the first word in a sentence will usually be capitalized automatically without having to go through this procedure just to do it.

Chapter 3 – Reading Books

The Kindle Fire HD, like every other model in the line, has the ability to display books of all sorts. You can use a few tips and tricks to make your Kindle Fire HD easier to use while reading whatever it is you want.

10. Change the Size of the Text

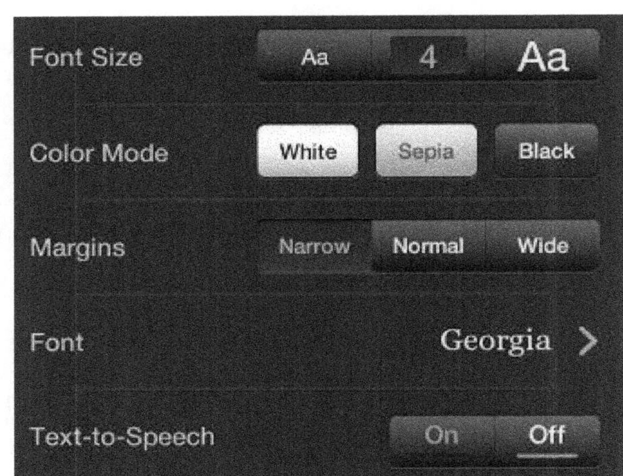

This tip will involve a different process based on the Kindle model you are using. This is what the menu will look like on the Kindle Fire HD.

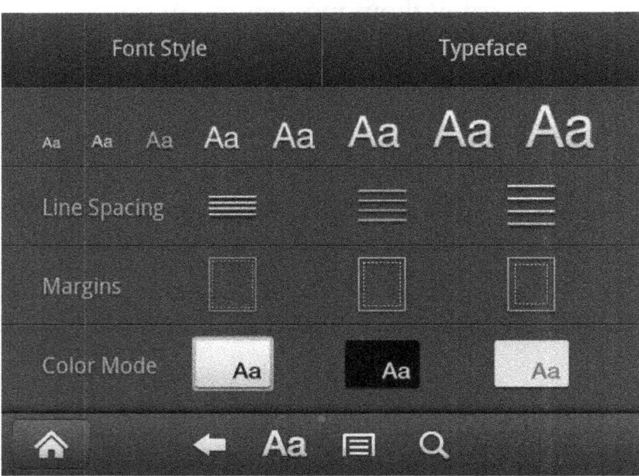

This is what it will look like on the regular Kindle Fire.

There are two ways how you can adjust the size of the text on whatever it is you are reading:

1. First, you can choose to open up the control menu by touching the Aa button at the bottom of the screen or at the top left part of the screen depending on the Kindle Fire model you are using. You will be able to adjust the font size based on the specific size you are comfortable with. There are

eight different sizes for you to choose from. The font size should be displayed based on the specific number that you are going to choose for setting up an appropriate size.

2. You could also use the traditional pinching or stretching finger motion on the screen. You can do this by moving your fingers closer together on the screen to make the text smaller or you can move them apart to make the text larger. This can be adjusted in the form that you see fit for whatever it is you are trying to read.

11. Change the Spacing

You can change the line spacing on your book by going to the Aa menu to make a few changes.

1. Go to the Aa control menu.
2. Look for the section that says Line Spacing.
3. Touch on the appropriate option to change the spacing based on what you prefer.

You will have three line spacing options to choose from. You can go with your choice of a single spaced option, a double spaced option or one that is a little in between.

12. How to Highlight Phrases

As the founder of Nerdism (your new object of worship), I have long been fascinated by productivity and what motivates people to achieve greatness. The Internet is the great equalizer. We all have access to the same data at all times, so there

You can highlight different phrases in your books as you see fit. These highlights will be used as bookmarks that you can access in the notes section of your book file. Here are a few steps for highlighting a phrase.

1. Tap the screen and hold your finger on the space that you want to highlight.
2. Drag your finger over the text that you are highlighting. The text that is being highlighted will be noted with a blue box around it.
3. A small screen should display asking you to highlight the passage. You can tap the Highlight button to save the text as a highlight.
4. You can now access your highlighted spot by going to your book menu and touching the View My Notes & Marks button. The highlight should be listed in this menu. It will be arranged in chronological order with the first few words in your highlighted spot displayed in the entry.
5. You can remove the highlighted option from the same View My Notes & Marks menu as you see fit. You can touch the option and hold your finger over it for a few seconds. This will open up a menu allowing you to either view or delete the highlighted passage as you see fit.

13. Highlighting Longer Passages

You can highlight long passages that you might not normally use on a standard display.

1. Highlight the text that you want to use.
2. Turn the screen from the portrait display to a landscape display. This should increase the amount of whatever you can display.
3. Highlight the rest of the text on the display screen by touching the screen near the spot that the highlighted area ended on.

This should allow you to highlight whatever you want even if it takes up two pages on a traditional portrait display. It is true that the book might look unusual when you read it on a landscape display but it doesn't take much for the Kindle Fire to figure out what orientation you are using.

14. How to Add Notes

You can add your own personal notes to a book on the Kindle Fire. The process of adding notes is similar to what you would do with highlighting phrases. However, it has a few differences to it because it involves the creation of new material that you can use for your reference.

1. Tap the screen and drag your finger over the text you will be making a note on. This is similar to what you would be doing when setting up a highlight.
2. Touch the Note button on the menu that comes up after you are finished choosing the text you want to emphasize.
3. A keyboard should appear at this next point. You can enter in whatever you want to add to the book through the easy to use keyboard on you screen.
4. Touch the Save button on the upper right corner of the keyboard when you are done entering in your note. The note should now be accessible from your menu.
5. You can edit the note later on by going to the View My Notes & Marks section of your book and then touch the appropriate note while holding onto the option. This will let you choose to either view, edit or delete the note as you see fit.

15. How to Share Your Progress

You can share your progress with a book with other people who are interested in hearing what you have to say about it.

1. Go to the book menu as you are reading it.
2. Touch the Share Progress bar.
3. Enter in the appropriate format that you want to share your progress in. You have the option to send your data to others through a traditional email client or through Google+ among a few other social media services.
4. You will then be asked the send a message to an appropriate recipient's account name or email address. This can be added in any format that the Kindle Fire is able to support when sharing this information with other people.

5. The body of the message can be edited as well. The standard message will say that you are at a certain percentage into a particular book. You can add things to that message as you see fit.

The purpose of this feature on the Kindle Fire is to let people know what you are doing with a particular book. It can add to whatever it is you are enjoying by letting you tell people with pride what you are doing.

Sometimes your message might even encourage others to take a look at whatever it is you might be reading. It's also a perfect feature for when you are looking to talk with others about the book you have been reading. Be sure to use this when it comes to introducing your book to other people who might be interested in it.

16. Controlling the Background

You can adjust the background of the Kindle Fire in one of two ways. These can be used to make your Kindle document easier to read.

1. You can choose to adjust the brightness of the Kindle. You can do this with the same standard control found at the top part of your Kindle. This is done to adjust the visibility of the Kindle as you see fit.
2. You can also adjust the background with the Color Mode option on the menu in your book. The background can be adjusted to include either a white, sepia or black background based on your preference.

17. Utilizing Bookmarks

DAVID COPPERFIELD (FORMATTED SPECIFICALLY FOR KINDLE)

preferred cork jackets, I don't know; all I know is, that there was but one solitary bidding, and that was from an attorney connected with the bill-broking business, who offered two pounds in cash, and the

The bookmark in this example is blue. This means that it has been saved. However, you can also choose to remove it with the process listed below.

A bookmark will allow you to save your progress in any book you are reading. This can be used with a simple procedure:

1. Touch the center of the page you are reading. This should bring up a small gray graphic on the top right corner of the screen.

2. Touch the sliver graphic as you see it. This will allow you to bookmark the page. You can tell that it is working if the graphic turns light blue.

3. The bookmark will then be accessible through the View My Notes & Marks page on your book file. This will include the first few words of the page alongside the specific page number or the percentage in terms of how far into the book this is listed at.

4. The bookmark can be removed by both holding and deleting the entry in the View My Notes & Marks page or by touching the sliver graphic on the page you bookmarked. This will cause graphic to go back to its original gray color.

This process can be used for as many bookmarks as you see fit. Just be sure that you are using the right number of bookmarks so you will not be confused when entering this information into your Kindle Fire.

18. Search for Specific Words

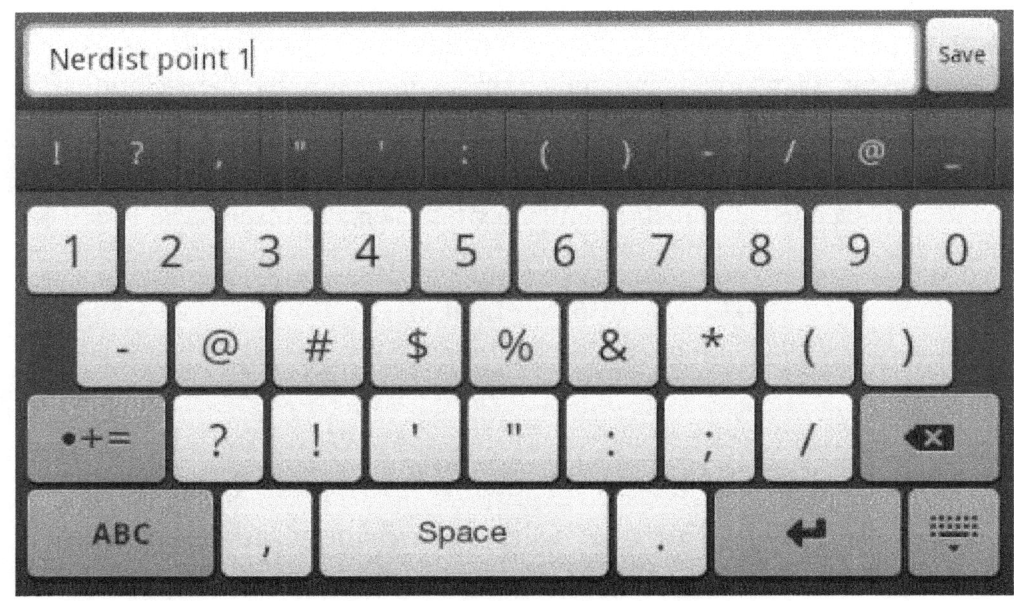

You can find very specific words in your Kindle Fire's book when you use this process for finding them. This is needed when you are trying to get into specific parts of your book. This can even be used with multiple words at a time to find certain phrases or names in the book.

1. Choose the magnifying glass icon on the book screen.
2. Type in the word that you want to search for. You should have the keyboard open at this point. You can open it by touching the entry box in the event that it does not show up the first time around.
3. Hit the Enter button. You should have access to all the instances where the word shows up.

You can also do the same if you find a word in a book and want to search for other instances where that word is being used:

1. Tap and hold onto a specific word in the book.

2. A few options will come up as you do this. You can choose the Search option to find other instances where this word is being used within your book.

19. Searching for Definitions

Sometimes a book you are reading will list information on any definitions you want to understand or get confirmation on. A book may have a link that you can touch to look up a definition so you can read it and then get back to the area you were on.

However, not every book has this feature. That's why you might have to search for a definition on your own. Fortunately, the dictionary feature on the Kindle Fire makes it easy for you to learn more about every single word that you could read. Here is how you can use this feature to find information on what certain words in a book mean.

1. Hold your finger on a specific word that you want to get the definition for.
2. Wait for the appropriate menu to show up.
3. Choose the option to look up the word.
4. The dictionary feature in the Kindle Fire will then guide you to the appropriate page where this word's definition is located in.
5. You should then close the dictionary so you can get back to the book you were reading.

20. Moving to Different Pages

You can move from one page to the next with ease:

1. Tap the center of the screen.
2. Hold onto the small circle at the bottom of the page. This should let you move to another page.
3. Hold the circle and move it to the left or right depending on the specific page you want to go to.
4. You can also use the table of contents feature on a book to move to specific spots on the book. This can include searching for the specific location in the book just as well.

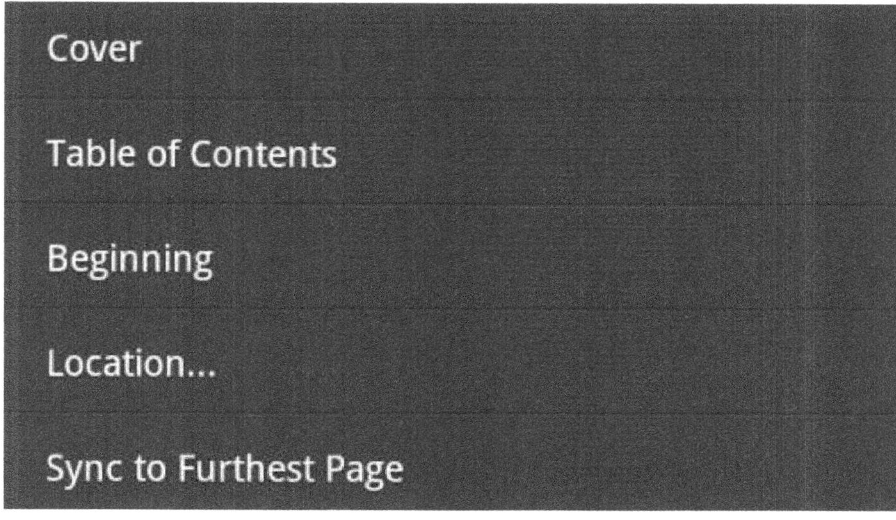

Sometimes your book might not have a set series of page numbers that you can use. You might have to just search based on the location that your book is in. That's why it helps to use the bookmark feature or to use the search methods listed above if you have a book that doesn't have a set series of pages on it.

21. Listening to Your Book

Did you know that the Kindle Fire HD has support for text-to-speech functions? You can use this to have the device read the book out to you.

1. Tap the screen as you are reading a book.
2. Go to the Settings section of the page.
3. Tap the Text-To-Speech option and choose to turn it on.
4. Push the play button next to the bar on the bottom of the screen displaying where you are. The speech will come out starting with whatever is on top of the page.

This feature is only available within the United States and only uses a digital female voice. Also, there are times where some pronunciations might not work as well as they should. This is due to the device running with a synthesized speech pattern.

You can always use an audio book through Audible instead. We'll get to that part of the Kindle Fire later on. However, it does cost extra to get an audio book. You can easily use the text-to-speech feature for free. There are obviously going to be some changes in pronunciation among other issues due to the ways how the synthesized speech program operates but it is still a good idea to think about what you might use in this case.

22. Sampling Books

You can read samples of select books to make it easier for you to see what might be available on the market for you to read. A sample will involve the first few pages of a book moving onto your Kindle. This is an easy thing for you to do when you use the right tips.

1. Log onto your Kindle account on the Amazon website.
2. Search for a book on the site that offers a sampling feature.

3. Click on the Send Sample Now button on the right end of the site.
4. Choose the device that you want to send your sample to. The Kindle Cloud Reader should be the default option for using this feature.
5. You should have access to the sample when you open up the book section of your Kindle Fire and then review the cloud section. The new download might be the first thing that will show up on your system.

You should use this to get a better idea of what's in a book. It can be a good way to gauge the interest of the book before you choose to buy it.

23. Renting Books

You can rent books for reading purposes if you use the right process. This can allow you to have a book for a certain amount of time and only pay a portion of the cost of using this book.

1. Select a book you want to rent from the book store on your reader.
2. Look and see if there is a Rent This Book option.
3. Choose an appropriate rental period through the calendar. This can last for as little as 30 days or as many as 360 days depending on what you would prefer to use.
4. The book will be in your possession when you confirm the rental period. It will no longer be in your possession after the rental periods ends.
5. Use the Manage Your Kindle page to extend any rentals that you might get.

The rental option is not available for all books. This is due to the rules that some copyright rules that some book publishers prefer to use.

24. How to Lend a Book

You can lend one of your books to another person who has any kind of Kindle Fire model or even another kind of reader. The book you send over will be available for fourteen days.

Loan this book

Loan this book with anyone you choose. Complete the following and click **Send now** to loan your book. The recipient does not need a Kindle to accept this book. (Learn more)

The publisher has set the following lending terms: this book can be loaned once for the duration of 14 days.

Your lending details * required field

Recipient E-mail address: *

Recipient Name:

From: * Charlie

Personal Message:

300 characters left

Send now

1. Go to the Manage Your Kindle part of the Amazon website from a larger computer.
2. Select a book that you have already purchased.
3. Click on the Loan This Title option.
4. Enter in the email address of whoever you want to send this book to. You can also add a personal message if you wish. You'll have to use the personal email address of whomever it is you are sending the book to and not a Kindle.com account.
5. You also have to enter in your identity when sending this book out. This is done to let your recipient know who is giving out this book.

Remember, you can only do this with books that you can actually rent out. There are some books that you cannot loan to other people due to copyright restrictions or because a publisher is refusing people the right to do this for promotional purposes.

25. How to Receive a Loaned Book

The process for receiving a loaned book will be different from the process of lending it. It is clearly easier to use because you don't have to buy something and then enter in a full email to get it all sent out. However, you do have to use an appropriate procedure for receiving such a book. This is easy to use no matter what you add to it.

1. Open the email that you received stating that you can get a book that someone is lending to you.
2. Log onto your Amazon.com account if you have not done so already.

3. Select the specific Kindle account that you want your book to move onto.
4. The book will be delivered to you through the cloud network. This means that it will stay there and will automatically be removed from your account within fourteen days after you receive it.

You have to make sure you respond to an email relating to a loaned book as soon as possible. You will have only seven days to respond to an email like this in the event that you do receive an offer for a book.

26. Getting Books From Public Libraries

A number of public libraries around the country have begun to include digital books in their selections. You can use your library account with one of these libraries to find one of many different books that you can rent for a period of time. You can use this process with both the Kindle Fire and the Kindle Fire HD.

This is a relatively interesting tip to use because it gives you access to more books of use. It links you up to books without requiring you to pay anything for them. Just be sure that you read your book on time because a digital book from a library, like any other book you might get from a physical library, will only be available to you for a limited amount of time.

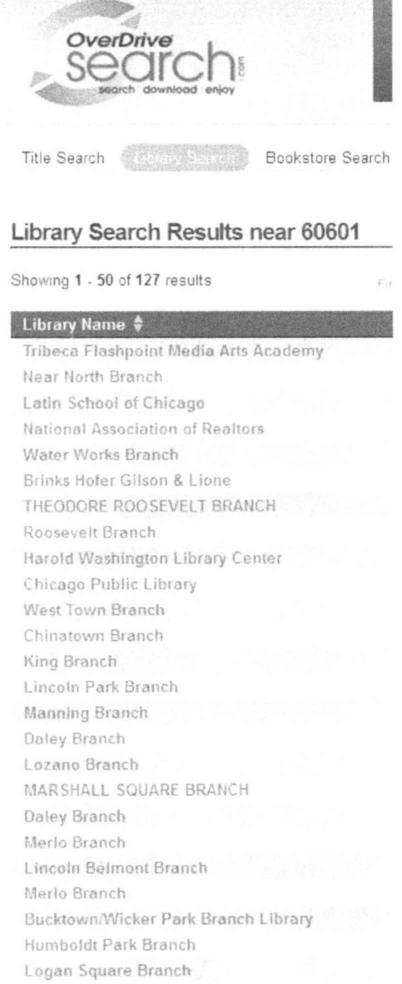

1. Go to the OverDrive website at search.overdrive.com. You can search for a library based on your zip code or by the specific country or local area that you are in.

2. Make sure you have the appropriate library card for whatever library you want to use. This card should include not only your name but also an appropriate PIN that lets you get access to your account. Be sure to keep this PIN somewhere so you can access it later on through a library website as needed.

3. Select an appropriate digital book on the website of whatever library you want to borrow from. You could get access to the library by clicking on the appropriate link for whatever library you prefer from the OverDrive website.

4. Log into the website of whatever library you want by entering in your card information and PIN.

5. Choose the appropriate link for reserving a digital form of the book you are interested in. The process of doing so will vary by each individual site.

6. Choose the Kindle file format on the site. You should be redirected to the Public Library Loan page off of Amazon.com. You will also be asked to log into your Amazon account at this point.

7. Choose the proper device that you will have the book delivered to.

8. The book will now be listed on your device for fourteen days.

You will have to use either a Wi-Fi connection or a USB connection depending on the book you are getting or the Kindle Fire model you have. The USB connection must be used in the event that you can't get on an appropriate Wi-Fi network. In addition, some books may only be moved to your Kindle Fire through a USB connection due to restrictions relating to a book. These restrictions are usually added by the publisher of the book.

27. Finding Public Domain Books

Start reading *David Copperfield* on your Kindle **in under a minute**. Don'

David Copperfield [Kindle Edition]
Charles Dickens (Author)
(312 customer reviews)

Digital List Price: $0.00 What's this?
Print List Price: ~~$5.00~~
Kindle Price: $0.00 includes free wireless delivery via ***Amazc***
You Save: $5.00 (100%)

- Length: 1108 pages (Contains Real Page Numbers)
- Don't have a Kindle? Get your Kindle here.
- Whispersync for Voice: Ready

Whispersync for Voice
Now you can switch back and forth between reading the K
audiobook. Learn more

Many older books are available in the public domain. It is easy to find these books off of your Kindle Fire.

1. Go to the book store on your reader or the Amazon website.

2. Type in the name of the book you want to use or the author of the book. You may also check the free book section to see what's available.
3. Select the Kindle version of the book. This should have no value attached to it.
4. You should be able to use the same one-click buying process to get this book. The only difference is that you are not actually going to be charged anything just to get this part of your book set up.

Be sure that you watch for the features that come with a public domain book. Some books that you might get off of the public domain don't have all the special features you'd come to expect out of a traditional book.

Chapter 4 – Using Magazines and Newspapers

The Kindle Fire HD will let you subscribe to and read magazines and newspapers of all sorts. There are a few tricks that you can use to give yourself more out of these publications.

28. How to Subscribe to Something

The appearance of the virtual edition might be different from what you get in your physical edition of the magazine. However, this might prove to be effective for whatever you want to read.

It's easy to set up a subscription to anything you want to read. Here are a few steps that are easy to use.

1. Go to the Kindle Store to find magazines or newspapers. You can search for them like you would with books or applications or anything else you could buy off of the Kindle Store.
2. Choose an individual publication based on what you might be interested in.
3. Check out by clicking on the appropriate icon for whatever you want to subscribe to.
4. The subscription should be registered and sent to your Kindle in a few hours. This is much better than a traditional print subscription in that those print subscriptions tend to take at least 12 to 16 weeks just to get the first issue sent to your front door.
5. You can then access the Subscription Manager on the Kindle website to review your subscription.

29. How to Renew or Cancel a Subscription

The Auto-Renewal Subscription feature will let you re-subscribe to different magazines or newspapers after your subscriptions run out. Amazon will give you a re-subscription at the lowest available price unless you cancel it. Canceling a subscription to avoid this charge is easy to do. However, you can also renew a subscription on your own if desired. This will involve a renewal with the set value that was established by Amazon for whatever you are using:

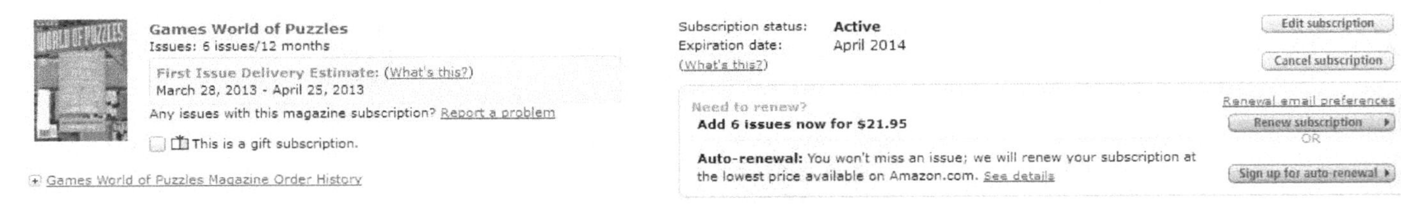

1. Go the Subscription Manager part of your account. You can do this off of your Kindle account on the Amazon website.
2. Click on the Cancel Subscription button.
3. You will receive a pro-rated refund of whatever issues you did not receive.
4. You can also choose to renew your subscription manually instead of having your subscription renewed automatically.

You should particularly do this in the event that your Kindle Fire has been stolen or is lost somewhere. You can do this to keep anyone from adding to your subscriptions outside of your permission. You can always choose to subscribe again to what you have later on and still get a pro-rated refund for what you did not get after your cancel it.

30. Moving Existing Subscriptions to the Kindle

Any subscriptions that you already have with physical newspapers or magazines can be moved to your Kindle without having to buy anything extra. You can even use this trick to get rid of the print copy of your subscription or to give you a virtual edition that goes in addition to your standard print one.

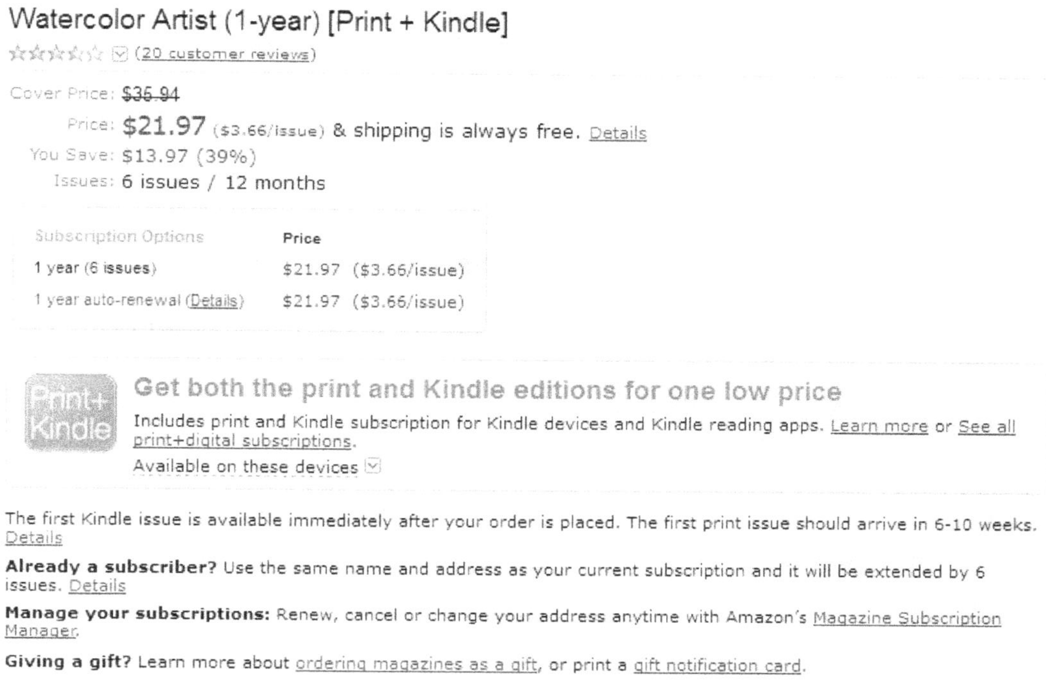

An interesting part of this is that you can add a Kindle edition of your subscription to go with your print edition. This can be used directly off of the Kindle or the Amazon website as seen above. You might even get a free extension to your subscription depending on what you are using.

This is a popular feature used to give you a quick look at what's available. Here's a look at how you can do this for whatever you want to watch:

1. Place on order for the magazine subscription through your Kindle or through the Amazon website.

2. Use the same name and address that you are already using on the shipping label on your newspapers or magazines. You have to use this info **exactly** as it is because the publisher will interpret your order as a renewal rather than a subscription if you use the exact information as it is read.

3. You will find details on the approximate arrival of your next new issue onto your Kindle. The Kindle will also read your current subscription and start to list information as needed.

31. Keeping Old Issues

The Kindle Fire HD will remove old newspapers and magazines in order to make room for new ones that you receive. It is all done to keep the periodicals from using up more hard disk space than what you might need off of it. Any issues that are at least seven issues back will be removed automatically. However, you can keep these old issues if you use this simple trick:

1. Open the issue of the periodical you want to save.

2. Click on the Menu icon.
3. Select the Keep This Issue option.
4. The word Keep will appear next to the specific issue. This means that the Kindle Fire HD will hold onto that issue for as long as you want to have it.
5. You can go back to the Menu for the individual issue and ask to delete it once you no longer have a need for it.

The issues that you choose to manually keep will be saved on your Kindle Fire for as long as desired.

32. How to Save Articles

You can save individual articles from different publications. This can be done without having to hold onto the rest of the periodical that you got the article from.

1. Open an article of interest.
2. Click on the Menu spot.
3. Got to the Clip This Article option.
4. The specific article that you have selected will be saved to your Kindle's drive. This will be used for as long as you want even if you delete the publication that you saved the article from.

33. How to Find Old Issues

You can always buy an older issue of a newspaper or magazine in the event that you never got one or your subscription to it started before that issue came out.

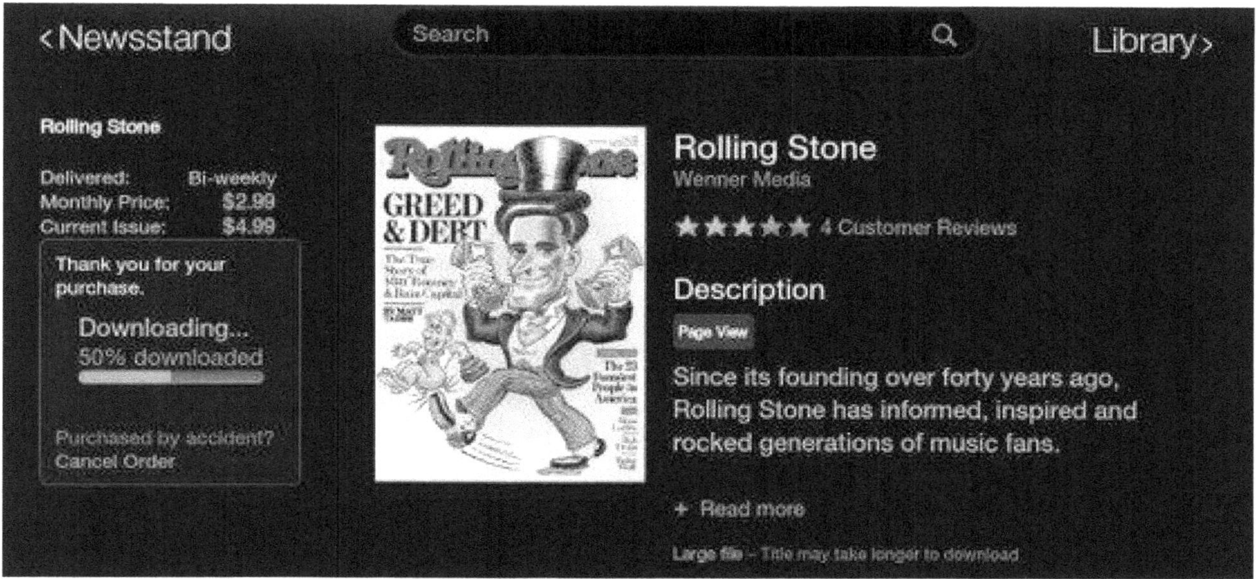

1. Open up your selection of newspapers or magazines.
2. Press and hold down on a specific selection.
3. You will receive an option to take a look at the back issues that are available. You can choose this to see what you can buy.

Remember, you will have to pay the regular non-subscription price for any back issue that you want to see. This is provided that the issue in question was not a part of your subscription to begin with. As you can notice from the picture above, the average cost per issue is going to be higher when you buy it outside of a subscription.

Kindle Format 8 is one of the most unique types of reading formats that you can use on the Kindle Fire or Kindle Fire HD. This is used to replace the .mobi file format that Amazon has been using for its Kindle book files for years.

The Kindle Format 8 style is made with the intention of displaying a book with a clear arrangement. It uses embedded fonts that can change in the book, support for a massive number of colors and even a plan to use multiple layouts within the same page. This is a feature that makes it valuable for people who want to read comic books, graphic novels, technical documents, some forms of fiction with alternative arrangements and even children's books. It can also display color pictures alongside text, thus making it perfect for cookbooks that show you pictures of the foods you can make by following certain instructions.

This section of the guide is dedicated to taking a look at how the features on this program can be used. This is made to give you access to more things that you can read on the Kindle Fire or Kindle Fire HD.

Basic Cupcake Bites

The cupcake pops are extremely popular, but these cupcake bites come in a close second. They rely on the use of a plastic candy mold to help form the shape of the cupcake bottom. No sticks. No tapping off excess coating. Just a neat, professional-looking finished product. And best of all, they're easy!

When visiting the candy-making sections in craft and cake supply stores, I began to pay attention to the various candy molds that are available. When I saw one for candy cups, I immediately thought it would be perfect to replicate baking cup liners. I love the ease of this method.

34. Reading .mobi Files

The format should be able to use .mobi files with ease. It will have to convert these old files into the new format to make it easier for your reader to use them right away.

1. Open up the old document that you want to read.
2. Wait for the document to be converted. It may take a few seconds for the Kindle Fire to read the document.
3. The document should be made available to use.

35. How to Zoom In

You can zoom into different items on a Kindle Format 8 file with this easy to use process. It certainly beats having to use the dragging motions of your fingers just to go in or out of an area.

1. Find the space that you want to zoom in on. This can include a block of text, a comic panel or a diagram.
2. Tap the space to zoom in on twice.

3. You can press the back button on your Kindle Fire or tap the screen twice again to zoom back out of the screen.

36. Playing Media Content Within a Book

There are some cases where a Kindle Fire book under this format can include a multimedia feature that allows you to play back different multimedia files of your choosing. You can do this with an easy process to get it all running right.

1. Touch the area that has the media link in it.
2. Press the proper play button.
3. The control should be the same as what you might use with a standard media player on your reader.

37. Adjusting Text

The text is a little harder to adjust on this format but it is still easy to use when you take a look at an appropriate procedure for maintaining it the right way.

1. Open the appropriate control spot for the book. This should have been read over earlier on in the guide.
2. Adjust the font size by using a larger or smaller text.
3. Check to see if the text is aligned properly or if some parts are not showing up properly. You might have to switch the Kindle Fire over to a landscape orientation if you are going to keep this running right.

Be sure to see what this file format can do when it comes to using a good format for reading your Kindle Fire books with. The format should be used to make it easier for you to read books with unique graphical features that you don’t always see everyday.

Chapter 6 – Playing Music

You can play a variety of music files on your Kindle Fire or Kindle Fire HD. The integrated media player in the Kindle Fire makes it easy for you to load and play back a file. It's also easy to find new files directly off of the Kindle Fire.

There are a few special tips and tricks to use when taking a look at how you can get a little more out of your Kindle when playing back files. Here are a few of the best tips that you can use when playing music on your reader.

Remember, **most of these tips are good only for those who get onto the Kindle Fire Wi-Fi network.** This is due to the extensive need that your Kindle Fire has for using a cloud system for accessing some of your files. It might be a leash to some but this is a necessity considering how you could get more music off of your cloud account than what might be placed onto your reader's hard drive.

38. Playing iTunes Files

The problem with Apple's iTunes program is that the files you download off of it are extremely restrictive. You only have a few ways how you can play these back or even place them on discs. However, you can play back the iTunes files on your Kindle Fire if you use these steps.

Select music to upload below, or browse for more music.

Music on your computer	Show previously uploaded music	# of Songs	Size (MB)
All music		346	1,814.3
Playlists		353	1,889.0
Artists		346	1,814.3

11 playlists and 1 song not included. View these items and learn about supported file types.

1 playlist and **346** songs selected to upload.

Estimated time remaining: **1 hour, 59 minutes**
Pause or exit at any time during upload. Learn more

You have **19.3 GB** of Cloud Drive storage available.
Your selections will use **1.8 GB** of this storage. Buy additional storage.

Start upload | Close

Portions of album art Powered by Gracenote

The cloud player can be used on a variety of computers.

1. Download the Amazon MP3 Cloud Player. This will allow you to upload your music onto the Amazon Cloud.
2. Go to the file folder on your computer where your iTunes files are located on.

3. Add these onto the uploading program. You will have a limited amount of storage space to use depending on what you have. In addition, it might take a while to upload everything onto the cloud based on how many files you want to upload.

4. Go to the cloud section of the music part on your Kindle Fire.

5. The songs that you uploaded onto the cloud should be fully accessible.

This is a very convenient feature but you have to be sure that you have enough data for whatever it is you are using. You have to not only be aware of the files you have but also the number of files you want to use. The Amazon Cloud will allow you to play back up to 250 music files. This can be expanded if you buy more storage for whatever what you want to get. Be sure to check and see what you could get out of your playback needs.

39. Playing Music in the Background

You do not have to keep the Kindle Fire music playback feature open at all times just to hear music. You can always use this playback feature while doing other things on the reader. The music will still be heard in the background. This might be useful if you want to multitask on this reader.

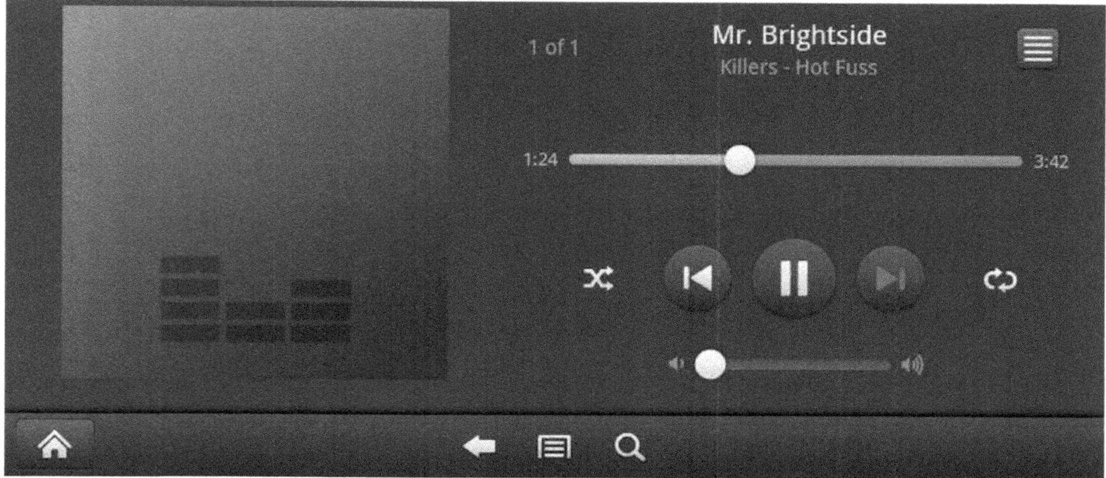

1. Press the home icon on the player at the bottom left corner.

2. Touch the gear button at the menu bar to reveal the track that is playing right now.

3. Press the gear button again after you are done adjusting anything that you want to play back.

40. How to Create Playlists

You can make your very own playlist that features a variety of songs that you want to listen to in some particular order. Here's how you can do this.

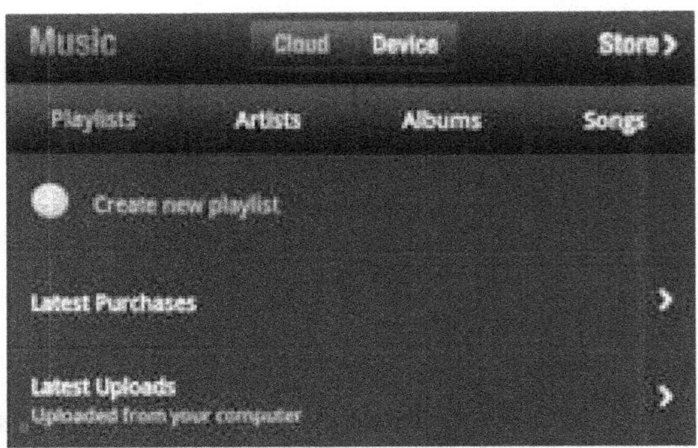

1. Link your reader up to a Wi-Fi network. You have to use this because all of your playlists will be added to the Amazon Cloud.
2. Go to the Playlists section of your Music menu.
3. Choose the Create New Playlist option on your reader.
4. Enter in the name of the playlist you want to set up.

5. Browser through all of the songs on you reader. This includes songs on the device and the cloud alike. You can also search for songs with the search feature on the reader.
6. Press the plus sign next to each track that you want to add to your playlist.
7. You can use the Edit button to move the tracks up and down on your playlist or to even remove some songs altogether.
8. The playlist can be loaded up later on and played back by simply pressing the appropriate name of the playlist on your reader.

41. How to Transfer Playlists

You can transfer playlists off of your Windows Media Player or Apple iTunes menu. Here's what you can do to play back these playlists.

1. Go to the Amazon MP3 Cloud Player as mentioned earlier in this chapter.
2. Search for the playlist files on your computer's hard drive. Try and look for files that feature songs that you know you will have access to on your reader or your cloud account.
3. Choose individual playlists and upload them as desired.

4. Your playlist will be ready to play back. Your list might end up skipping tracks in the event that you don't have the songs that correspond to the playlist or if you have those songs but they are in formats that might not be properly supported by the Kindle Fire.

The best part of this is that you can do this with just about any computer you might have access to. The cloud system will read your items from any computer and will let you adjust what you have provided that you have access to your account.

42. Using an Equalizer

You can use an equalizer to adjust the settings of your music files. This includes adjustments based on the bass, treble and other features. You can use this procedure for changing the ways how your sounds are being played back.

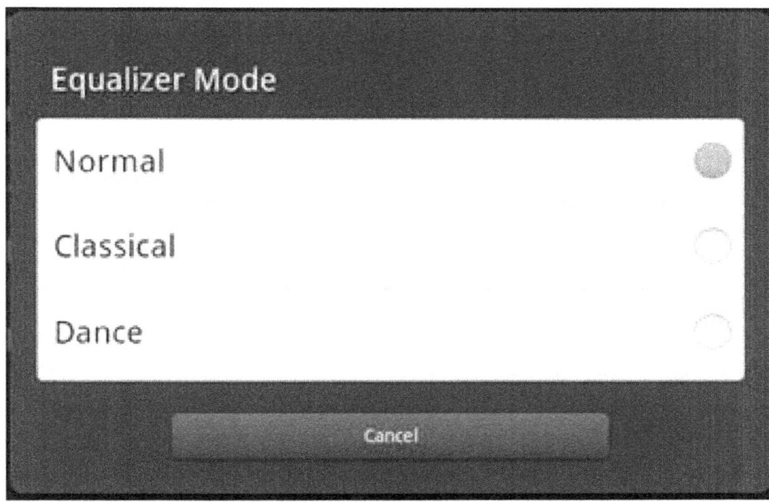

1. Go to the Settings section of the music part of your Kindle Fire. This should be at the bottom of the screen.

2. Go to the Enable Equalizer Modes section of the settings page.

3. Choose the appropriate setting that you want to add. You can use a standard mode but you can also use a Classical mode for more atmospheric music or a Dance mode for high-energy sounds that feature a greater series of bass tones.

This is relatively limited in terms of what you can do but you can always choose to download a separate equalizer application on your Kindle if you wish to do this. However, it may cost money for you to get one of these programs depending on what you want to use. It is a bothersome issue but it may end up being the best way for you to adjust the sounds on your Kindle Fire outside of what comes with the standard equalizer on the reader.

43. How to Stream Music

More people are streaming music on their mobile devices than ever before. You can do this with the Kindle Fire by using this process.

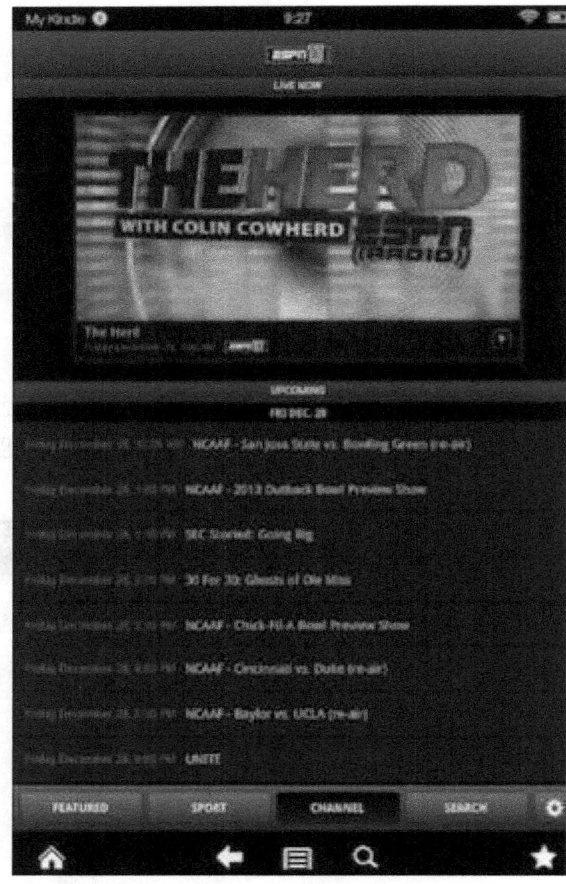

1. Open up files on your cloud storage drive and play them back as desired.
2. Another option would be to go to a website that streams music and download an appropriate playback application that might be used on the site. You can do this by entering in an appropriate website and opening up the player like what you see at the top of this tip.
3. Open the file and allow the radio to play back whatever it is you might be interested in using or whatever you already know how to play back.
4. Stay within a Wi-Fi network to get access to your files. The program will not work if you don't have an appropriate connection that lets you get onto your cloud drive.

There is also the option to use an application on your Kindle to load up streaming radio stations from all around the world. Be sure to search online to see what's available so you can do a little more with your Kindle. Fortunately, you should not have to deal with too many requirements just to play the files back.

Chapter 7 – Video Playback

It is easy to play back videos on your Kindle Fire or Kindle Fire HD. You can do this with a variety of video files but just remember that your file format options will vary based on what you can use. This should be seen well to give you a plan for entertainment.

The Kindle Fire HD will clearly have support for HD files. The standard Kindle Fire option is not going to feature the same option. You could technically download HD files for the standard Kindle Fire but they will just play back as standard definition files. Therefore, you are better off being aware of what your device can read before you actually download something. (And remember, it usually costs extra to get the HD version of a video versus the standard definition version.)

44. Fast Rewind

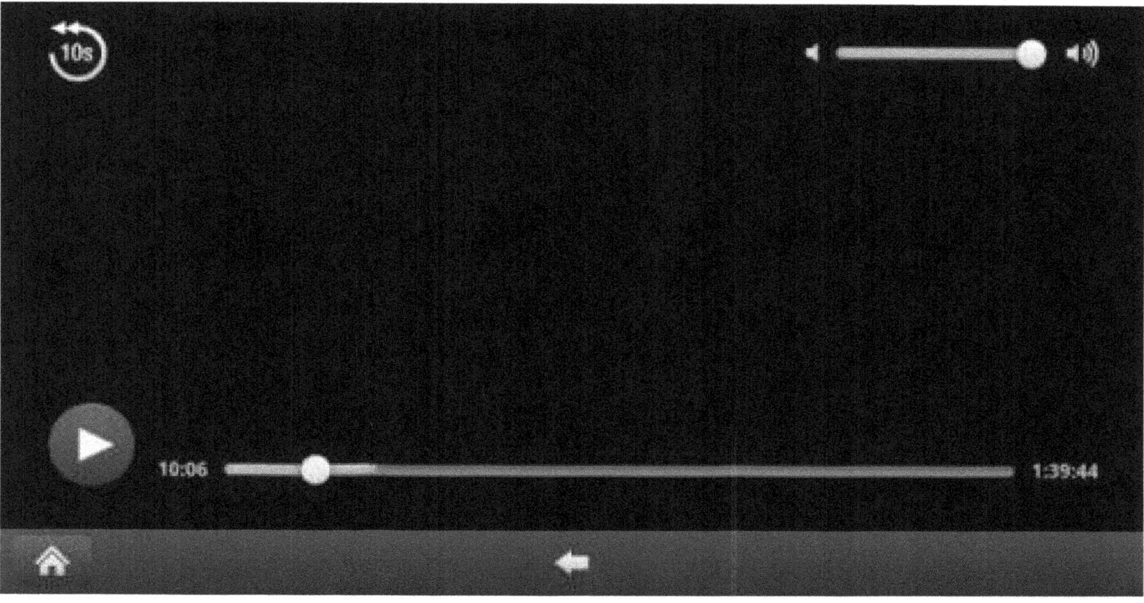

You don't have to struggle with a bothersome process to rewind the video back by a bit. You can use the fast rewind feature to adjust the video playback to where it will be easier for you to see what you are playing.

1. Tap the middle of the screen while a video is playing.
2. Tap the top left part of the screen.
3. The video will rewind by ten seconds when you tap this part.
4. Tap the button a few more times if you want to go back by about twenty to sixty seconds.

45. Using Whispersync

The Whispersync feature on the Kindle Fire is made to let you link your videos up to other devices. This means that you can set up details on where you stopped a video so you can play it back from that spot later on through another device. This can be used with an Apple iPad, a Microsoft Xbox 360 or Nintendo Wii U game console or one of many newer television sets of Blu-ray disc players.

1. Move the Kindle Fire near the device that you want to play your video file back on. This should be made with the same Wi-Fi connection on both devices.
2. Connect the device to your Amazon Instant Video account.
3. Log into the account and open up the file that you were playing earlier. It should be open at the same spot that you were on earlier.

This should be used well to give you access to your videos from more places. Naturally, you will have to watch for how the controls can vary between your Kindle Fire and another device that you are accessing your videos on.

46. Move Videos Onto Your Device

You can stream or download videos on your Kindle Fire with this process:

1. Go to the Amazon Instant Video section of the Amazon.com website. Make sure you are logged into the email account that your Kindle is attached to.
2. Click on an appropriate movie of interest to you.

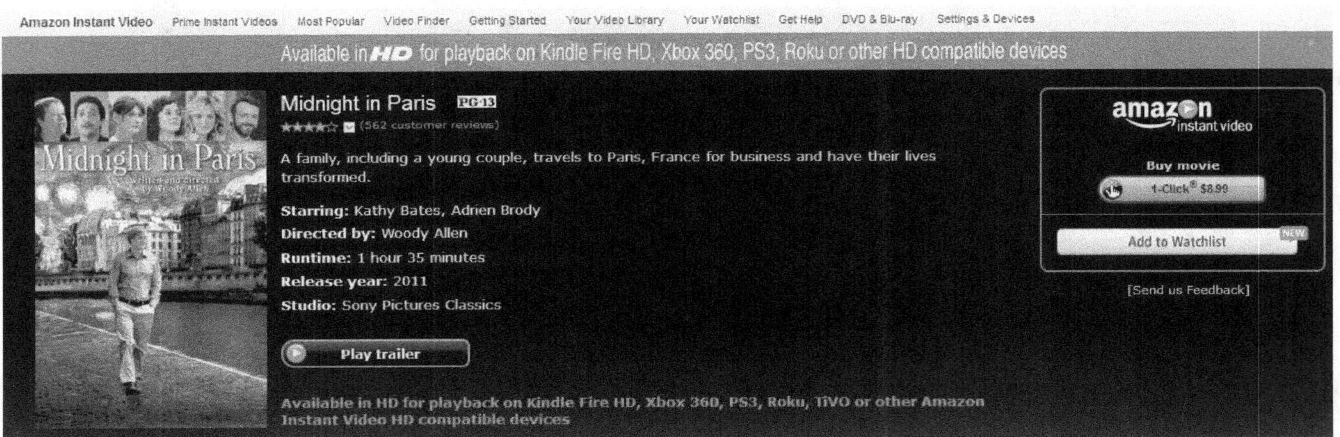

3. Choose the 1-Click option for downloading the video. You will have to pay to get the rights to this movie. Some other videos may be available for rental instead but the selection that you will have in this case will be relatively limited.

This should give you access to your files on just about any special device that you want to link up to. These include not only your Kindle Fire but any other device that uses Amazon playback features. Always check on the particular file that you are using when figuring out what is available for your use.

47. Reading Amazon Prime Videos

You can quickly get Amazon Prime videos set up as well. Just remember that **you have to use an Amazon Prime account on your name if you want to get access to all of these videos.** You can get a free trial for one month but it will cost extra for you to hold onto this account for longer than that.

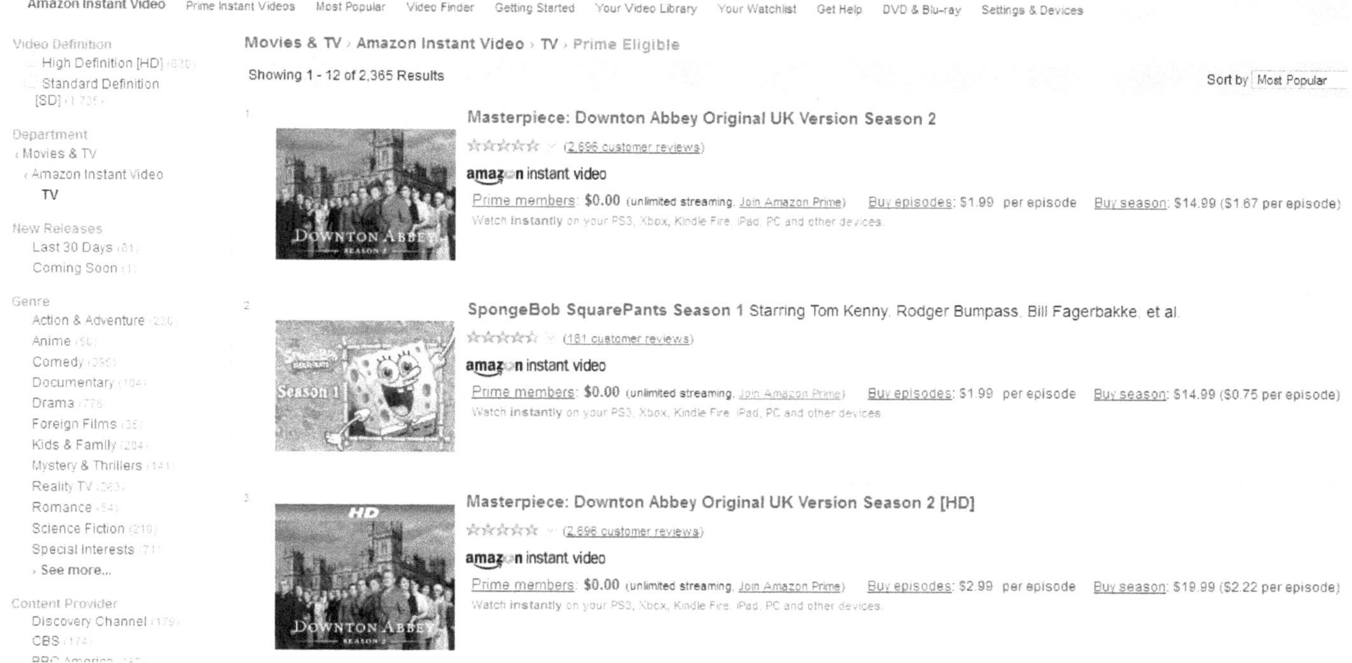

1. Go to the Amazon Prime website.
2. Click on the proper Prime Instant Videos section of the Movies and TV section.
3. Click on any selection of your choice.
4. You should have a selection of episodes to use. You can download as many of these as you want to view.
5. The videos can then be opened on your cloud account separately. You can also add them to a playlist in a way similar to what you use for your music files.

Remember, you cannot just download these files and hold onto them for as long as you want. You will lose access to the Prime video files you use if you lose your account or it becomes inactive. Fortunately, you can use the easy 1-Click purchase option to take care of your account when finding something of use.

Chapter 8 – Using Media Files

Not every media file format is going to be supported by the Kindle Fire or the Kindle Fire Hd. Therefore, you have to use a few ideas when finding a way to play back these files. This section features details on all the ways how you can use media files on your Kindle Fire even if they are not actually supported by your reader.

Most of these procedures will require you to download special applications onto your computer. They will be used to change the files you have into versions that can actually be supported on your reader.

48. How to View Unsupported Video Files

The Kindle Fire does not support AVI, WMV, FLV or MKV formats. However, you can get your Kindle Fire to support them by using these steps.

1. Install an appropriate video conversion program onto your computer. Pavtube is a good example of a program like this.

2. Select a media file on your hard drive.
3. Click on the Format section and select Kindle Fire. This should go towards the MP4 option.
4. Click on the Convert button.
5. Attach your Kindle to your computer and move the files that you have created from your hard drive onto your Kindle. They should now be ready to be played back as desired.

49. How to Use iTunes Files

iTunes downloads are protected with DRM controls. You can remove these controls so you can move these files onto your Kindle. You'll have to use this process for doing so.

1. Use an iTunes conversion program on your computer. ChewTune is the program used in this picture above.
2. Select the iTunes download of your choice.
3. Choose the Format you want to use. Be sure that the format is one that is actually supported by the Kindle Fire. The standard MP3 format might be the safe way to go.
4. Convert the file you have selected.
5. Move the file onto your Kindle after you connect it to your computer.

50. How to View Flash Files

You have to adjust your browser if you want the ready to actually play back your Flash files. This is especially needed in cases where you are going to websites that heavily utilize Flash. However, you can always choose to keep it on demand so you can choose not to load it at times and let the site load a little faster.

1. Open the Silk browser on your reader.
2. Tap on the menu and go to the Settings section.
3. Look for the Enable Flash spot.
4. Choose to select Always On or On Demand depending on your preference. The On Demand option will give you the choice to choose if you want to operate the Flash application on a file or if you want to avoid it.

This has to be done appropriately because the Amazon Kindle Fire HD will not play back Flash files in its default form. You have to adjust the settings on your own. Also, it is best to use the Silk browser if you are actually going to view Flash files on the Kindle. Fortunately, you don't have to install any new programs just to do this.

51. Moving Music on a Cloud

It's best to use the Amazon Cloud if you want to move music files onto your reader.

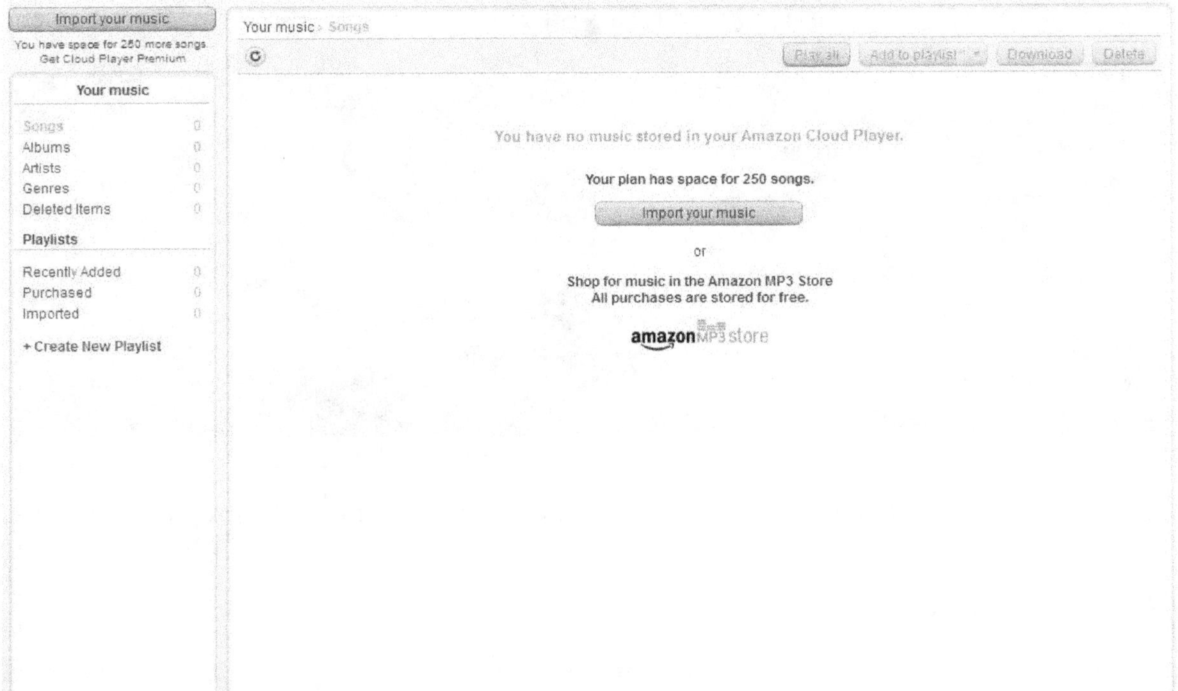

1. Log onto the Amazon Music Importer from amazon.com/cloudplayer. You can use your Kindle account to log in.
2. Click on the Import Your Music button.
3. Choose the appropriate files you want to add to the Cloud. You can get **as many as 250 songs uploaded for free. It costs extra to use more.**

4. The files should be accessible on the Amazon Cloud. They can be found on your reader by going to the Cloud section of your Music menu.

This can work well provided that you are careful with regards to how much data you have to use on the device. There are limits over what you can add based on how much space you have to use.

52. Using a USB Wire Transfer

You can move files directly onto your Kindle by dragging and dropping them with a USB wire transfer. This can be used with any kind of USB wire including one that might come with your reader.

1. Use an appropriate USB connector that is compatible with your reader. It should attached to a computer with Windows Vista or later or Mac OS X 10.5 or later.
2. The Kindle should then appear on your computer as an external hard drive.
3. Open the Kindle drive file to see what folders are available. You will have to determine which folder is appropriate for whatever you want to move around.
4. Drag the file or files you want to move from your computer onto the appropriate folder in your reader.
5. The files should now be readable on your Kindle as you go to the appropriate library section.

The videos that you move will appear in the **Gallery** section and not in the Video section. The only videos you will find in the Video section are ones that you bought off of the Amazon Video store. Fortunately, the videos will still be easy to load up and can be found with the same standard procedure for doing so.

53. How to Compress Video Files

You may want to compress some of the video files on your Kindle Fire HD if you want to avoid using too much hard disk drive space. This may particularly be the case when trying to conserve data by moving a file from an HD form to a standard definition form that takes up less space.

This procedure can work on both files on your reader and files that will move into your cloud. This helps because your cloud account has a limited amount of space for files just as well.

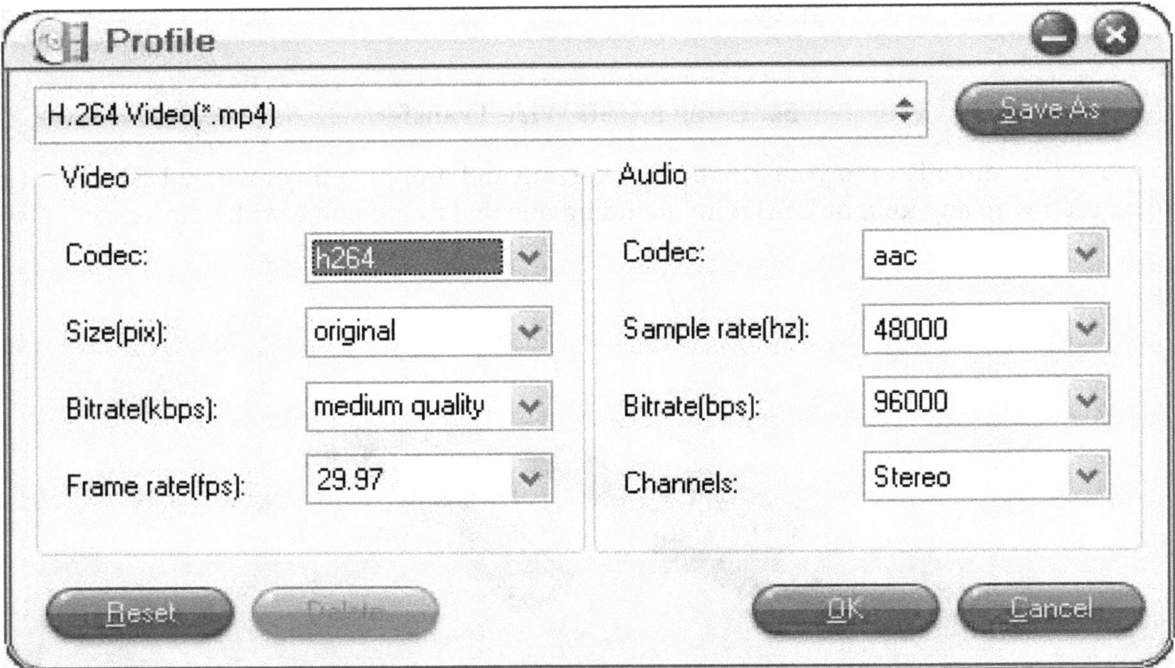

1. Move a video file from your reader onto a computer. You have to use a USB connection to do this.
2. Open an appropriate video conversion tool like the Pavtube tool mentioned earlier. You can see this on the picture right above.
3. Open the file and adjust the settings as needed. This includes adjusting the bit rate as needed. For example, a bit rate of 2000 kbps will be fine for most Kindle Fire HD models. Older models that use the Kindle Fire HD 7.0 system can use 1500 kbps.
4. Convert the file and move it back onto your Kindle. The file should be smaller in size if you have reduced the bit rate. Again, you have to get a USB connection set up so the file can go back onto your Kindle drive. You could also upload it to the cloud player if you would prefer to do that.

It's better to reduce the bit rate on your Kindle than it is for you to adjust the resolution in pixels or the frame rate. The bit rate refers to the number of bits processed per second. It makes a much higher impact on the size of a video file than the resolution. In addition, the loss of quality is nowhere near as visible with a lower bit rate as it is when the resolution or frame rate is changed around.

54. Attempting to Receive Converted Files the Second Time Around

There will be times every once in a while where you attempt to receive a converted file but it does not actually work. You can fix this problem with a few tricks. Be sure to use all of them to fix the problem that you might have.

1. Check the email address that you are sending your converted files with. The email address should be listed among the approved emails on your Manage Your Kindle account on the Amazon.com website. You will have to add your email address to the listing if it is not on there.

2. Check on the format of the converted file. It has to be something that can actually be utilized by the Kindle Fire.

3. Look through your spam folder in your email account. Sometimes a file that you need will be emailed to you but it will land in that folder because your email server does not recognize the person who sent that email to you in the first place.

4. Check and see if your Kindle Fire is actually within the range of a network. You have to use some kind of connection to a network if you want this to work. This is regardless of the type of network you are trying to get onto.

The conversion process has to be used with the right file format in mind. Be sure to compare the files you are trying to convert with the files that you have on your reader as it is. You should figure out with a simple comparison whether or not the files you are trying to convert should be used with specific formats in mind.

In some cases the file transfer will not work at all no matter what you try to do. The odds are the file will have been corrupted in some way and cannot be transferred. You might have to create a new edition of the file just to get it sent out to your Kindle.

Chapter 9 – Using Audible

Audible has become a popular service from Amazon for audio books. The site makes it easier for people to listen to audio books while on the go. You can use your Kindle Fire for the intention of downloading and listening to these audio books. You can use the Audible program to do a variety of things to give yourself a better experience with the Kindle Fire.

55. Adjusting Playback Speed

You can control the playback speed on the Audible application to a speed that might be easier for you to listen to. This can be supported by doing the following:

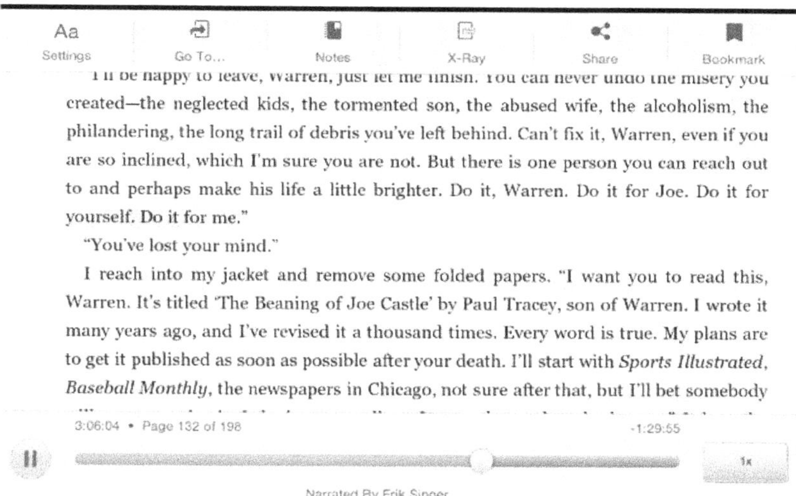

1. Go to the Settings section of the application or the spot on the bottom right corner of the screen.
2. Tap the Narrator Speed choice if you choose to use the Settings spot.
3. Adjust the speed based on your general preference. This can involve either half the speed of what you usually get or three times the speed.

This can help you out if you are trying to fast forward the book in some way.

56. Controlling Without Buttons

You can control the Audible application without the use of any buttons. This will give you an easier sense of control around the application.

1. Go to the Settings spot and choose the Button-Free option.
2. You can tap any part of the screen to pause or play the file.
3. Swipe left to go back by a few seconds. The distance you will go will vary based on what you have set up in the same Settings menu.
4. Swipe right to go forward by a few seconds. This will also be based on what was entered in the Settings.
5. Swipe up or down to go to the next chapter or to go back to the previous one. The file will go to the beginning of whatever chapter you have moved into.
6. You can hold your finger onto the screen for an extended time to create a bookmark. This will be used to list the time that you want to go to when referring to a particular part of the audio book.

57. Adjust the Sleep Timer

You can use the sleep timer to shut off the playback after a certain period of time. This might be useful considering how long an audio book might be. After all, some audio books might include several hours of a book.

1. Open the Settings menu on the book.
2. Go to the Sleep section of the menu.
3. Adjust the sleep timer based on how long you want the book to go on for.

Be sure to consider this with your battery life in mind. Sometimes the audio playback might create more pressure on your battery because it takes so long for something to play back.

58. Use Whispersync

The Whisersync feature on the Kindle Fire is made to give you access to your audio book with ease. This can be done with this simple process.

1. Buy the standard Kindle book.
2. Buy the Audible file for the same book.
3. Start by playing the Audible file or by reading the Kindle book.
4. You can switch over to the other format after a while when you use the Whispersync feature.
5. This should work as long as you keep the Kindle Fire on your account and that you stick with a secure Wi-Fi network when using this feature.

Chapter 10 – Using the Wi-Fi Network

The Kindle Fire's Wi-Fi support is strong because it links your Kindle up to just about any place in the country where you can get access to the Wi-Fi network from. Here's a look at what you can do in order to get into this powerful network from any place that you want to use your Kindle in.

59. How to Identify Networks by Security

You should be sure that you check on the details of your wireless networks by looking to see which ones are available for you to enter into and which ones have to be controlled by adding some password.

1. Open the Wi-Fi menu on the top of the screen.
2. Check on each individual network to see what is listed here. Look and see if there is a padlock listed on any of these networks. The ones that have a lock on the network logos on the left hand side are the ones that you have to add passwords into so you can get them to work.
3. Tap any network without a padlock on it to open a window stating what the security process is like and what encryption may be used. You can choose to connect to that network from there if you are interested in doing so.
4. Tap the network listing with a padlock to enter in an appropriate password for access. This type of network should have more protection than what you'd get out of a public network.

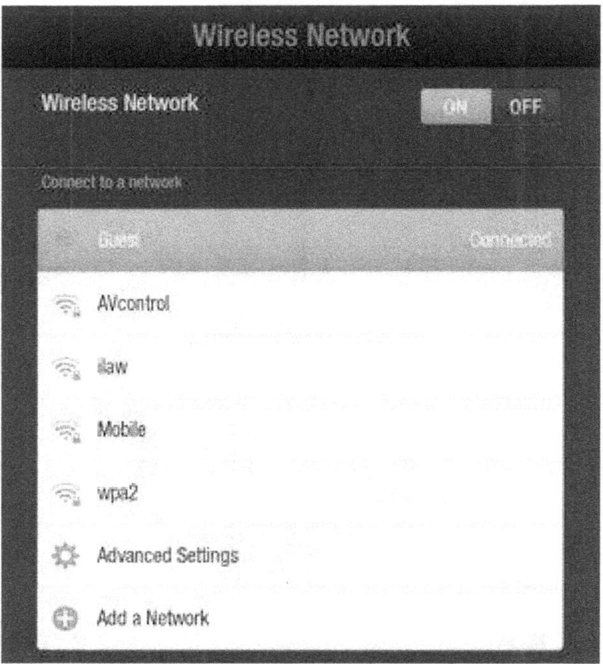

As this example shows, a majority of the networks here are protected. The Guest network is the only one that is not actually connected with a secure connection in mind.

60. How to Add a Wi-Fi Network

Your Kindle will automatically review all sorts of Wi-Fi networks where you are. However, there are times when the network you want to get access to can't be found on your reader. That's when you have to manually add a Wi-Fi network to your reader. Here is a look at how you can do this.

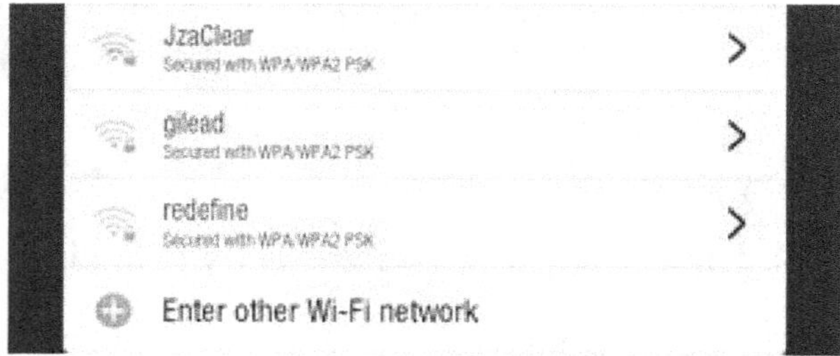

1. Go into the Wi-Fi menu on the top bar of your screen.
2. Choose the Add a Network or Enter Other Wi-Fi Network option on the screen that lists the Wi-Fi networks in your area. Be sure that the Wireless Network option is on before you do this.
3. Enter in the name of the network you are trying to get access to. This is also referred to as the Network SSID.
4. Enter in the encryption information on your network. You may have to enter in an appropriate password to get access to the network in the event that the network you are getting into is private.
5. Enter in the password if necessary.
6. Choose the Save option to save the information about this network onto your reader.

7. Touch the Connect button to reach the network. It might take a bit for the reader to acknowledge and get you onto the network of your choosing.

This process should be useful for most Wi-Fi networks. These include most WPA networks and even 128-bit WEP networks.

61. Forgetting Networks

The Kindle Fire HD will remember the networks that you connect to so you can get access to them later on as needed. However, you also have to option to forget any networks that you have gotten into. This can be done by removing the data about certain networks from the Kindle Fire as needed. Here's a look at what you have to do in order to keep the Kindle from automatically connecting to a certain network you've used in the past.

1. Go into the Wi-Fi menu.
2. Check and see if the Wi-Fi network you want the device to forget about is on the screen. It has to be in your local area if you want to get the device to forget about this network.
3. Tap on the specific network you want the reader to forget about.
4. Choose the Forget option on the password entry screen.
5. The Kindle Fire will now remember to get you onto a different Wi-Fi network instead of the one that you chose to forget about.

This should be useful in order to keep your reader from trying to stick into a weak network that is not being run properly. It could be used well to prevent you from using more battery power by trying to keep on connecting to a network.

62. Fixing Problems with a Connection

Sometimes your Kindle might not link up to a Wi-Fi area where you are in spite of other devices linking up to it just fine. You can fix this problem with a simple procedure.

1. Press and hold onto the power button until an appropriate screen comes up.
2. Choose the Restart option when it appears.
3. The Kindle Fire will have to restart. It will take a few minutes but it should be more likely to find the Wi-Fi network in your area after you restart it.

These are simple methods but they can be used to protect your network. These should be made to give your Kindle Fire the access to an online network that it deserves.

63. Fixing Wi-Fi Interference

Sometimes additional items in an area might interfere with Wi-Fi signals. These include radio and television signals. Your Kindle Fire can be fixed with these procedures:

1. Adjust the antenna for the television or radio that is causing the problem. This might be done to keep the signals that come into the area from getting in the way of your Kindle.

2. Move further away from the television or radio signals. This can improve the potential for your Kindle Fire to work without any problems.

3. Move the outlets for your devices if necessary.

Don't forget that weather conditions might create Wi-Fi interference as well. High winds or precipitation are often issues. Ice can also be problematic in the event that an outdoor antenna is covered in it. This could cause some signals to reflect off of its surface, thus keeping you from getting your tablet online.

64. Entering a Password

You should not have a tough time with entering in a password for your Kindle Fire's Wi-Fi access. Here is a step by step process of doing so.

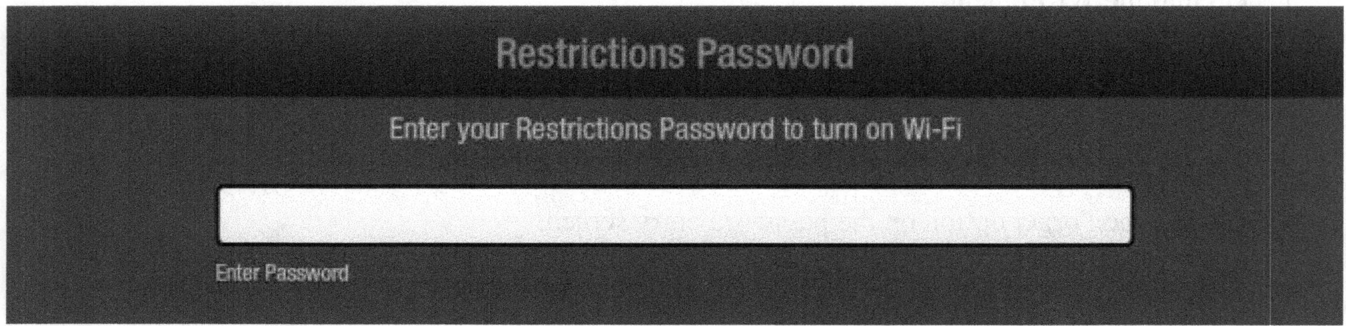

1. Tap the appropriate network that you want to get access to on your Wi-Fi menu. This should be a protected network if you have to get a password entered into it.

2. Enter in the appropriate password that you should have written down elsewhere. This information should have been provided to you by a local wireless connection provider.

3. Check on the specific type of network that you have to enter into. This is a guide that tells you how long the password you have to enter might be. For example, a 64-bit WEP security network should have a 10-digit password while a 128-bit WEP network should have a 26-digit password. A WPA password can be at least eight digits long and may include phrases if needed.

4. The reader should be able to connect to the Wi-Fi network provided that you enter in the appropriate keyword for getting onto the spot you want to enter.

65. Creating Password Coverage

One option for using a password on the site is to use a password for connecting to an online network. Here are a few things to do in order to create a password for online use. This password will go well beyond the standard password that you might have to enter when getting access to the network in the first place.

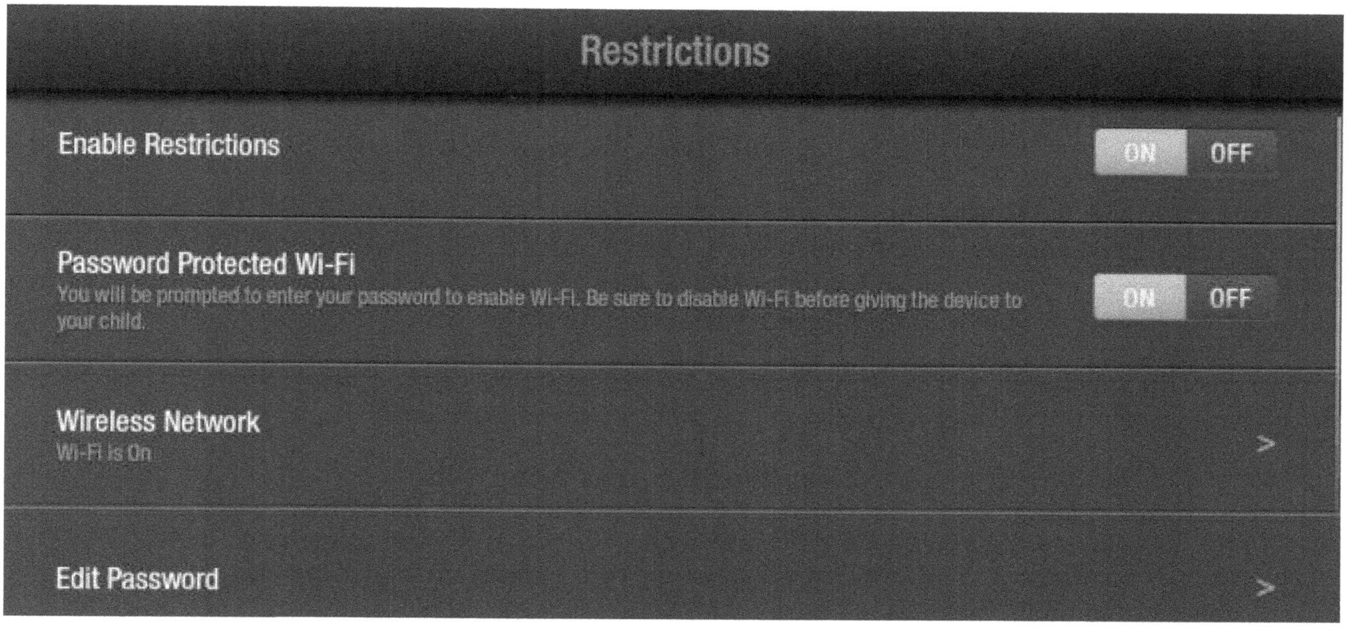

1. Go to the Settings feature on the Wi-Fi menu.
2. Use the Restrictions menu on this spot.
3. Choose the Password Protected Wi-Fi option.
4. The Kindle Fire will require you to add a password onto your reader before you can open up the Silk browser. This means that the rest of the device can be accessible but the online functions cannot be used unless the right password is added.

You can add to the protection that you are giving your kids when you use this feature in the reader. It is made to keep your reader running right.

66. Syncing with Servers

The Kindle Fire has to sync up with servers in order to use the Wi-Fi network to download files. You can sync up with servers by doing the following in the event that you cannot get onto a server at a given time.

1. Turn off the Wi-Fi feature.
2. Restart your reader altogether by using the process mentioned earlier in this book.
3. Turn the Wi-Fi feature back on when it starts up again. Be sure to find the appropriate network that you want to download your files onto.

Chapter 11 – Battery Saving Tips

While the battery on the Kindle Fire HD is convenient, it does not last forever. The battery can work for about eleven hours on average off of a full charge. The amount of time it will last will be highly influenced by what you are doing with your reader. In fact, the device will use more battery power when you use it for high-level activities like playing back video files.

You can use the follow tips and tricks for keeping the battery on your reader under control. These ideas should be used to make it easier for you to get your device up and running.

67. Controlling the Apps Being Run

Sometimes the battery power on your Kindle will wear out faster if you are using more applications than what you really want to use. You can find out what apps are running on your Kindle so you can stop certain apps from running, thus making it easier for your battery to relax for a bit.

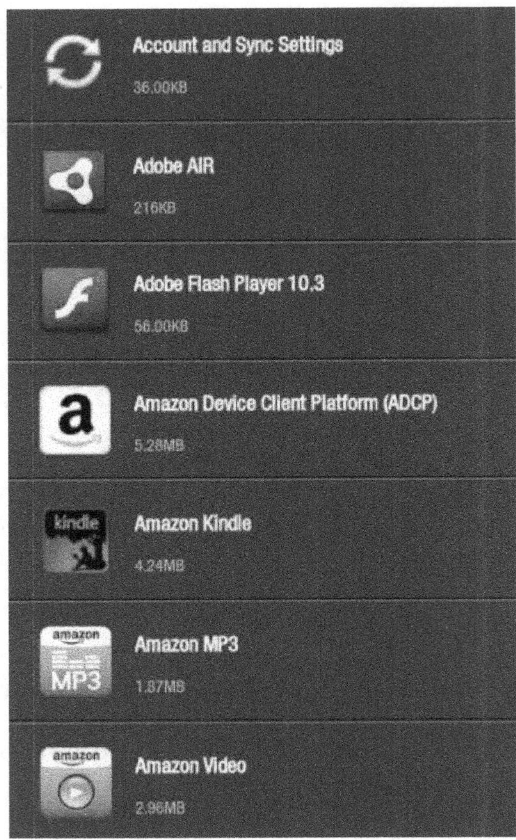

1. Go to the Settings section of your Kindle.
2. Use the Applications section of the Settings menu.
3. Touch each individual application that you do not want to run. You can choose the Launch by Default option to set up an app to run as the Kindle starts up or to keep it from starting.

4. The Force Stop feature may also be used to stop an application as it is running. This is often used in cases where an app is causing problems with your Kindle but you could also use it for cases where you want the Kindle to stop running at some time.

This may be useful if you have applications that take up too much space on your Kindle. After all, sometimes your Kindle might have applications that you running in the background without you even knowing that they are running in some way.

68. Turning Off Wi-Fi

While the Wi-Fi feature on the Kindle Fire is convenient, it is also a feature that will use up more battery space because it involves keeping your Kindle online. You can turn it off whenever you are not using a wireless network or you are not accessing anything off of the Amazon cloud.

1. Go to the Settings bar on your Kindle.
2. Select the Wi-Fi option on the top. You have to touch the Wi-Fi button at this point.
3. The Wi-Fi option should be turned off at this point.

69. Turn Off Cloud Access

Part of fixing your battery issue is to turn off access to the cloud network.

1. Avoid loading any application or file listed on the cloud network.
2. Use a USB connection on a computer in the event that you are trying to get on the cloud in some way or another.
3. Be sure to keep the Wi-Fi signals on your device turned off.

70. Observing the Wi-Fi Signal

Your battery is more likely to die out if you keep trying to get your device to connect to a Wi-Fi network. A reader that attempts to sign onto a wireless network with a weak signal will be more likely to use battery power in its attempt to get online. You should do the following to keep this from being a hassle.

The Wi-Fi signal can look like this. This will feature a few bars going from the bottom to the top. A network with more bars is easier to connect to than one that does not have enough bars.

1. Look for a Wi-Fi network that has at least three bars of strength on it. This should be much easier to get onto.
2. Avoid using networks that keep dropping in and out.
3. Turn the Wi-Fi feature off in the event that you can't actually find a strong enough network that will stay online for a while.

71. Controlling the Brightness

The brightness feature on the Kindle Fire will adjust the visibility of the screen. This is useful for many cases but a brighter screen will result in the Kindle using more battery power just to illuminate what you have. You can use the following tips for controlling the brightness.

1. Go to the control bar at the top part of the Kindle.
2. Select the Brightness section to bring up an appropriate bar.
3. Adjust the total brightness on the Kindle by adjusting the bar to the left or right as you see fit. You have to move it to the left if you want to keep the brightness under control with a lower amount of battery usage.
4. Try to lower the brightness level to the lowest possible total that it can get. This means that it should be completely dim. In fact, you should not have much of a problem with viewing it if you have a good natural source of light to use alongside the tablet.

You may want to check on the brightness of whatever space you are using your Kindle in. This could be used to determine whether or not you really need to have all that light on your Kindle. Remember, a device that uses a brighter setup will end up using more battery power because of the added energy used to keep the light running.

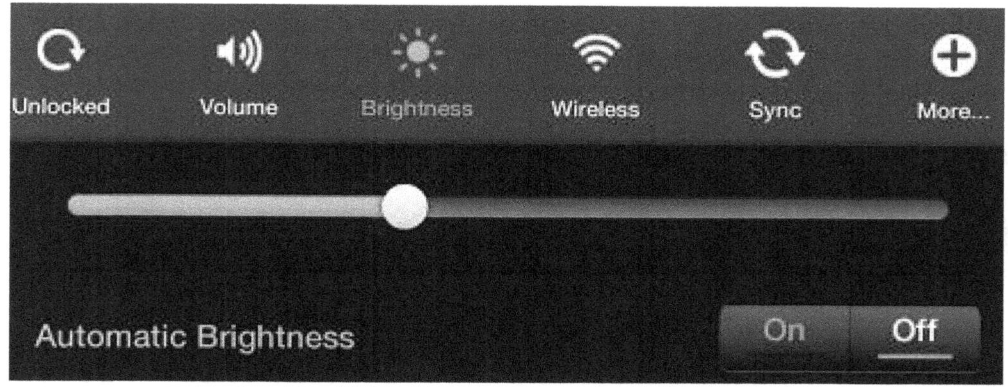

72. Turning Off Automatic Brightness

The Automatic Brightness feature is also made with a design to help you keep your brightness under control.

1. Open the Brightness section of the Kindle Fire.
2. Choose Off on the Automatic Brightness section.
3. This should allow you to have more control over the brightness of the Kindle Fire because it will not adjust itself depending on what it uses.

This should be used carefully so you can keep the Kindle from sensing the brightness levels in a local area. Your device will use less energy if you can keep its brightness controls from being as strong as they could be.

73. Using Sleep Mode

The Sleep Mode feature is used to conserve battery power by keeping it from using energy but not by turning off the Kindle.

You can use this in the event that you want to keep the Kindle from using energy by keeping all its applications and functions off. Meanwhile, the Kindle will be easy to start by up as soon as you activate it again because the device will not turn off altogether.

Here's a look at how you can use the Sleep Mode feature on your Kindle Fire or Kindle Fire HD.

1. Touch the appropriate power button on your reader.
2. Quickly release the power button after touching it. You should not hold onto it for too long or else it will shut the device off altogether.
3. The device should then go to black. It should not display any additional messages. These messages would only show up if you hold onto the button for too long.
4. Touch and release the button again to get the Kindle out of Sleep Mode.
5. Enter in any passwords that might be added to your Kindle. This is all based on whether or not you actually added in a password a while ago.

Remember that the power button on the Kindle Fire will vary in its appearance based on the model that you have. The picture listed here is a display of what the Kindle Fire's power button looks like. A similar button should be used on the Kindle Fire HD.

74. How to Set the Reader to Lock

You can lock the reader so it will turn off after a while. This is where the reader will go into Sleep Mode automatically after a while. This is provided that the reader has not been in use for any purpose after a period of time. You can use this feature to make sure it does not use more energy than what it has to use.

Here's a look at how you can set the reader to this particular feature:

1. Go to the settings bar and touch the More option.
2. Control the setting that states how long the Kindle can be used for. This includes setting the Kindle based on how much time it will take for the device to go into Sleep Mode after a while.
3. You can turn the device back on by touching the power button.

75. Disabling Location-Based Items

The location-based materials on your Kindle might be useful but they can take up plenty of battery life. This is due to how the Kindle can read your location based on the Wi-Fi networks you are using. Fortunately, you can disable these location-based items by using a few easy to use steps.

1. Go to the More section of the settings bar on the top of the Kindle.
2. Go to the Location-Based Services menu.
3. Turn off the two options in this menu. These options relate to the general location-based services on your Kindle and the Google search support for keywords and identifying information based on where you are located.
4. Avoid opening anything that might read your location as well. These include map applications or even phone directories among a few other items.

76. What is Airplane Mode?

Airplane Mode is a feature that will shut off many of the connecting features on the Kindle Fire HD. This is traditionally used on airplanes where wireless communication devices have to be shut off so they will not interfere with the communications features on an airplane.

This should be used to keep the device running without any online connections. It will be controlled through the same Wireless menu as what you use for getting your Wi-Fi connection set up. You will have to turn off this Wi-Fi connection just as well.

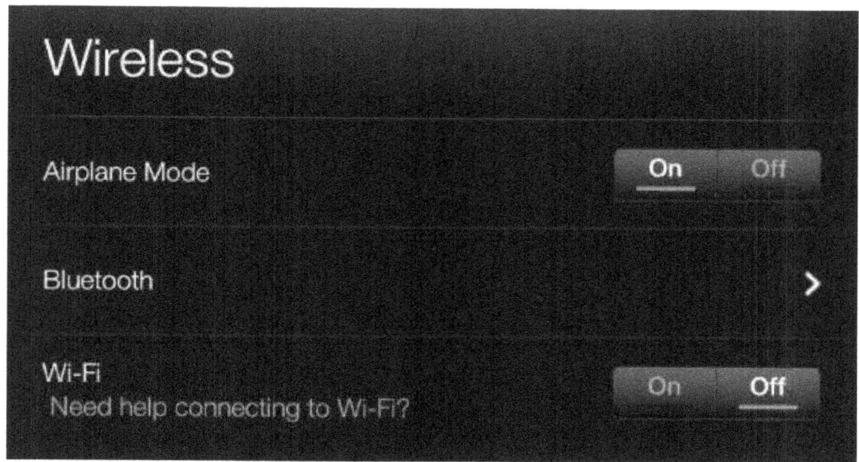

This can be used even if you are not on an airplane. You can use it to keep your Kindle from using too much battery power by using online functions. Here's a look at how you can activate Airplane Mode.

1. Go to the Wireless section of your settings bar.
2. Select the On option on the Airplane Mode icon.
3. The connection features on your Kindle should automatically turn off. This includes the Wi-Fi connection support system. They will go back on when you turn Airplane Mode off.

Note: Airplane Mode is referred to as Aeroplane Mode on Kindles based outside of North America. It is still the same thing no matter where it's used.

77. How to Stop Images From Loading Online

It takes longer for a website to load when it has images. Additional battery power is also required when using these images. You can tell the Silk browser to stop loading images so you can save battery power.

1. Open up the Silk browser.
2. Go to the Settings menu.
3. Look for the Load Images option in the Advanced settings menu. This should be found near the bottom part of the menu.
4. Remove the check mark from the Load Images box.
5. The Silk browser will stop loading images until you put the check mark back in.

78. How to Turn Off Email Syncing

Email syncing is used on the Kindle to make it easier for your email accounts to be accessible on your Kindle. However, this feature can take up battery power. That's because your Kindle will constantly check on the email servers your accounts are in. It will check on your email every fifteen minutes to see if anything has loaded up.

This will use battery power that you might not be able to afford to use. However, you can turn off email syncing by using a simple procedure for doing so.

1. Go to the More section of the settings bar.
2. Go to the Application section in this spot.
3. Choose the E-mail, Contacts, Calendars section.
4. Tap on the appropriate account name that you want to adjust. This should be the email that your Kindle is wired to but you could also have multiple accounts on there depending on what you have been doing with your Kindle in the past.
5. Go the Sync and Data settings section. You can choose to turn off the options to sync your reader up with your e-mail, calendar and contact features.
6. You can also change the frequency of how often your Kindle will check for messages if you want to keep this feature on. Just go to the Inbox Check Frequency feature and adjust the timing to where the Kindle Fire will wait a little longer before it tries to check your inboxes again.

79. Controlling the Audio

Did you know that your Kindle Fire HD can use battery life just by using its external speakers? The energy needed to get those speakers set up can be a challenge. Fortunately, there are a few steps that you can use to keep the audio on your Kindle Fire HD from being more of a hassle to your battery than it has to be.

1. Adjust the volume by tuning it down or even muting it as needed. You can do this with either the standard volume control buttons on the side or by using the control screen on the top of your reader. The option you have will be dependent on whether you have a Kindle Fire or Kindle Fire HD.
2. You can add headphones to the appropriate jack on the side of the Kindle Fire as well. Just be sure that you use them responsibly and with the right safety standards in mind.
3. Adjust the stereo or mono features on the audio. This might be used to control the audio to make it easier for the Fire to be read properly.

80. How to Appropriately Charge Your Kindle Fire

You should do the following when recharging your Kindle Fire. This should be done to make it easier for the device's battery life to go on for as long as possible.

You can do this with either the standard charger that goes into a wall or by linking your Kindle Fire up to a computer through a USB connection. You can also use a car charger; we will talk about that a little later on in this guide.

1. Watch for the battery life on your device. Wait until it is close to being out of power before you recharge it. You can wait until it reaches the 10% mark before doing so.
2. Plug the reader into an appropriate charging outlet.
3. Wait approximately three to four hours.
4. You can then remove the reader from the charging unit after this time ends.

You should do this because the Kindle Fire will remember its battery capacity at a better rate if you recharge it with the right standard in mind. Also, the reader will not be forced into too much pressure if you keep it from being charged up as the battery is full.

81. Checking USB Ports

One helpful idea to use for keeping your Kindle Fire running well is to see that you are using a safe USB connection. However, a USB connection might not work very well when it comes to charging up your reader.

When you see this screen, you will know that your Kindle Fire is hooked up to a USB port. This means that it will be charging itself. However, sometimes you might struggle to get the USB port to actually charge up your Kindle Fire.

You may need to use a few additional tips when finding a good solution for fixing the problem. Here are a few of the things that you can do in order to fix this problem so your Kindle Fire can charge right.

1. Check and see how well the Kindle Fire is charging itself when using the USB connection. You might have a problem if it is not responsive. This may especially be noticeable in the event that the reader does not actually charge itself up properly within about two to four hours like it should be able to.

2. Try to move the connection to a different spot. You could use a USB port on the back end of a computer if a port on the front end is not sufficient enough for your charging needs.

3. Check on the quality of the USB connection. The ports on the USB wire might be rusted or dirty.

   You will have to clean this connection off with an air can or a small cotton swab to get rid of any debris that gets in the way. It is often easier for the USB cable to develop stuff inside of it than it is for the ports on your computer to develop this debris.

4. Be sure you don't use anything on your Kindle Fire while charging it up. It takes longer for the device to charge up when it is operational.

   In fact, you might be better off keeping the reader on the off switch while charging it. The screen that you see at the top of this tip will still appear on the reader even if you have turned the Kindle Fire off before you started to charge it up.

5. Check on the quality of the ports on your computer. Sometimes a port might end up being jammed due to an issue relating to something like dust or other kinds of debris. These may naturally occur on any computer over time.

   You might have to use an air can to remove some of the debris in these ports provided that the air can is not too intense and does not harm any of the other components in your computer.

You should make sure that you adjust this feature in order to make it easier for your USB connections to link up well. You have to get the ports running right.

82. Turning Off Dolby Support

The Dolby sound system on select Kindle Fire models is useful but it also takes up more battery power than what you could afford to use. Be sure to do the following:

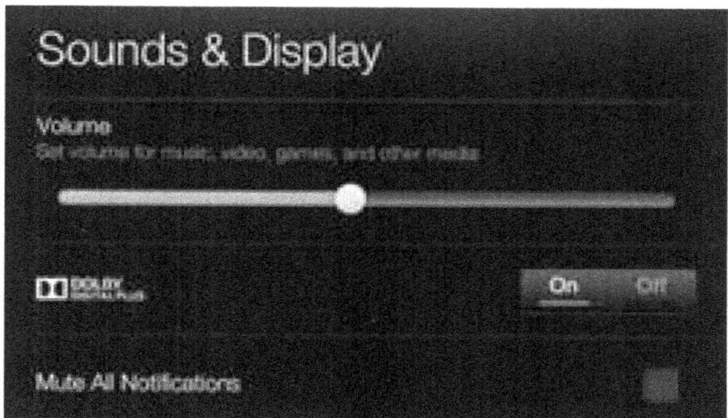

1. Go to the Sounds and Display section of the Settings menu.
2. Turn the Dolby system off. You can find this near the top part of the menu.

This is an extension of the earlier suggestion to control the stereo or mono quality of the audio. This has to be adjusted even more because Dolby sound support takes up more battery space than even a standard form of audio control.

Chapter 12 – Application Tips

Your applications are important to your Kindle Fire. They are what make your device all the more functional for anything you want to do with it. You can use these tips and tricks to make it easier for you to enjoy all your applications.

This section involves the use of many applications that are used on the Google Play store. This is the store that Amazon supports on its Kindle Fire devices.

This comes from how the Kindle Fire is run with some support from the Android operating system. This operating system uses the Google Play format for getting its applications set up as well as the Android programming language to get the applications to run on your reader.

In fact, you can use a particular process in this section to find third party applications. While it is true that you can find loads of different apps off of the Kindle Fire, this support for third party apps will only add to the value of your reader.

83. How to Buy Apps

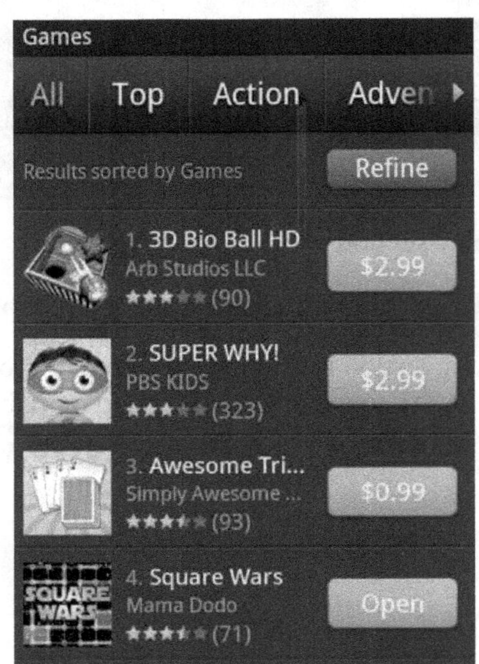

1. Go to the App Store section of the Kindle. This should be found under the Apps section of the top of your Kindle.
2. You can then search for an application to buy based on either the section you want to visit on the site or by entering in a keyword.
3. Tap the entry for an application.
4. Tap the yellow button that lists the price of the application to download it. The cost of the application will be automatically added to your credit card or whatever you have linked your account up to. However, you can also download an app for free if you see that it is listed as free without any prices attached to it.

84. How to Arrange Your Apps

You can arrange the applications on your Kindle Fire by what you might prefer.

1. Go to the Apps section.
2. Tap either the By Recent or By Title option.
3. You can also hold onto an icon and drag it from one part of the app menu to another.

This should allow you to arrange your apps based on how you want to view them.

85. How to Download an App from a Computer

You don't have to add an application directly from your Kindle Fire HD. You can always go online and download an app to your reader off of a larger computer. You can connect your device to a computer or you can choose to upload an app to the cloud network instead.

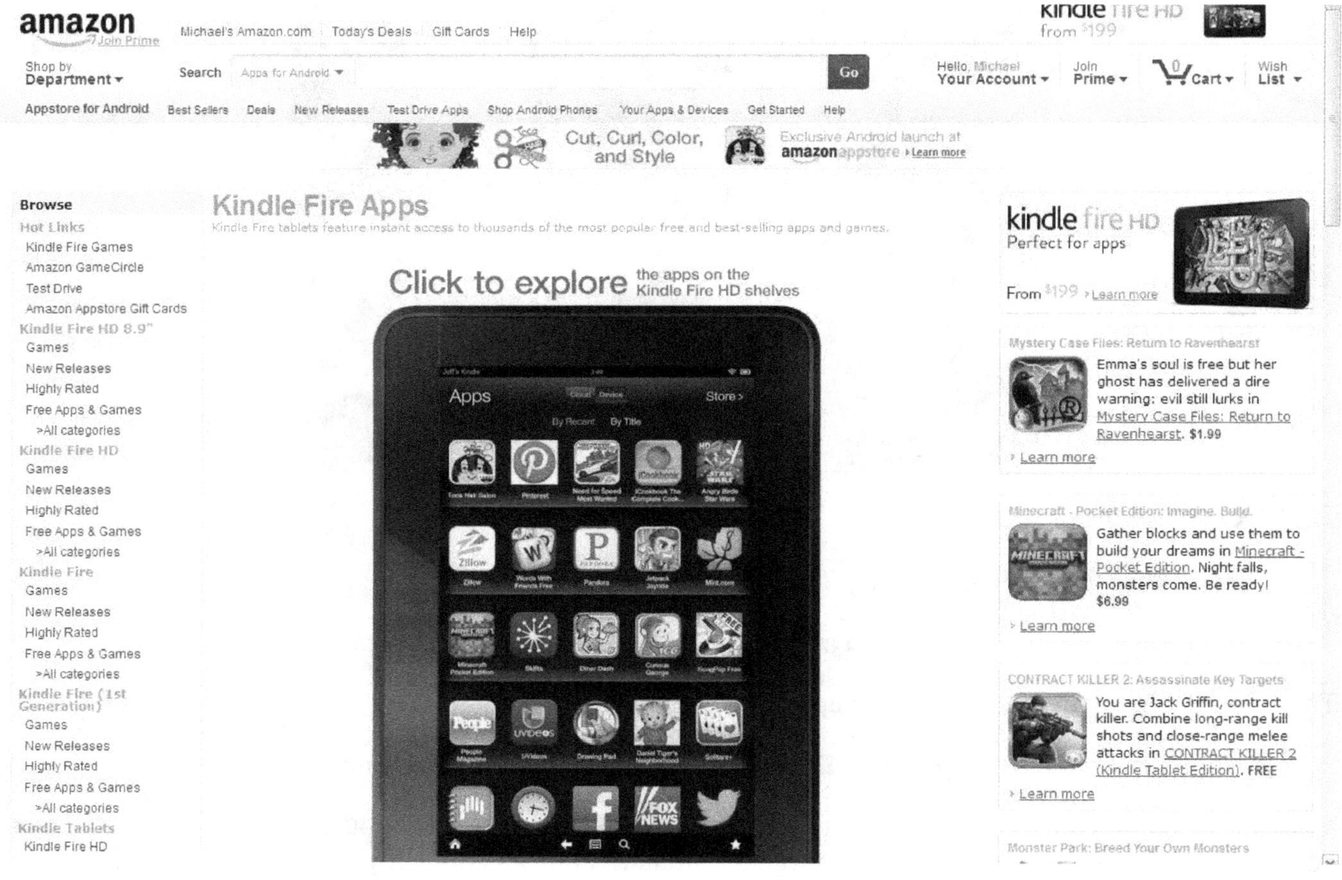

1. Go to the App Store off of the Amazon website. You should be logged into your account as you are doing this.
2. Search for application off of this site. You can do this by searching through the bar at the top of the browser or through any of the links on the left hand side of the menu.
3. Buy the applications that you want to use.
4. The applications should be loaded up to the cloud network. Your Kindle Fire will download them as soon as it starts up again but you can also choose to keep them on the cloud so you can download them later on as desired.
5. You can also link your new app directly to your device's hard drive by attaching your reader to the computer through a USB connection.

86. How to Find Updates

Not all apps on your reader will update themselves automatically. Here are a few things that you need to do in order to update your applications as needed:

1. Go to the Menu section of the App Store.
2. Select the My Apps option.
3. Check and see on this part of the Kindle what updates are available for your individual apps.

Each individual application has its own schedule for releasing updates. Be sure to check for these updates accordingly.

87. How to Delete an App

You can delete applications from you reader in the event that you are trying to free up space on your reader. This simple procedure can be used to give you easy access to a plan to get rid of anything you do not have a need for.

1. Go to your application library.
2. Press and hold onto an app that you do not want.
3. Tap the Remove from Device prompt as it appears.
4. The app will be uninstalled from your reader.

88. How to Reinstall an App

The apps that you uninstall from your reader will be easy to access off of a simple download off of your reader. This can be done with a simple process.

1. Go to the application library.
2. Tap on the Cloud section of the library. This should have a listing of the many apps that you have downloaded in the past regardless of whether or not you have uninstalled them.
3. Tap on the proper app that you want to reinstall.

There are times when the data that was originally on your app will not be retained after you reinstall it. Sometimes the data that was saved in an app might be deleted from your reader altogether when you uninstall it the first time around.

89. How to Load Apps at the Start

Sometimes you can get an application to load up on your Kindle Fire right as you start up your Kindle. There are a few things that you can do when setting it up right.

1. Open up the Settings menu.
2. Enter the Applications section of the Settings menu.
3. Tap an application and choose the Launch by Default option.
4. You can restart your Kindle Fire or shut it down and then start it up again. The app you specified for this process will start up automatically it boots up.

This procedure is best suited for applications that might run in the background. They should not be all that invasive provided that nothing is too problematic.

Be sure to also watch for how the application is set up with regards to data use. You can tell how much data a program is using by taking a look at the number of megabytes listed next to the name of a particular app.

90. How to Arrange Apps as Favorites

You can arrange the apps on your device by using a few simple steps to control the ways how they are being displayed. Part of this involves adding a special spot where your favorite apps will be listed above a number of others. Here's how you can adjust your apps to where you will create a section dedicated to nothing but your favorite applications.

1. Hold down on the item you want to add to your favorites.
2. Wait for the screen to show an option letting you to add something to this section. Choose that option when it appears.
3. You can access the item later on by going into the Favorites section of the front page on the Kindle Fire.
4. You can delete these items from your favorites later on by holding onto the item in your Favorites section and choosing the option to remove it from there when it shows up.

91. How to Sideload an App

Sideloading is a process where you can install a third party application onto your Kindle Fire. This can include an application that you cannot get off of the store.

This is a procedure that is made to keep your reader more functional. In addition, you do not have to root your device at all in order to use this. Here is how you can sideload an app onto your reader.

1. Download the ES File Explorer program onto your reader. This should be free to install and should be found right off of the store on your device.
2. Install the program and then go to the Settings part of your Kindle Fire.
3. Click on the Device section of the Settings bar.
4. Go to the option that allows you to install applications from outside sources. Choose the on switch for this option.
5. Connect your Kindle Fire to a computer with a USB cable.
6. Copy all the APK files for items that you want to install onto your Kindle Fire.
7. Open the ES File Explorer so you can get access to a series of file folders and individual files.
8. Touch the icons for any applications that you want to install.

Now that you know how to get a third party app loaded up, you can go online to find them. The process for doing so should be the same as what you might do elsewhere when finding apps for your benefit no matter what you are interested in using.

92. How to Get Third Party Apps

You can find many third party apps to use on your Kindle Fire as soon as you are done setting it up for sideloading purposes. This can be done with a few steps.

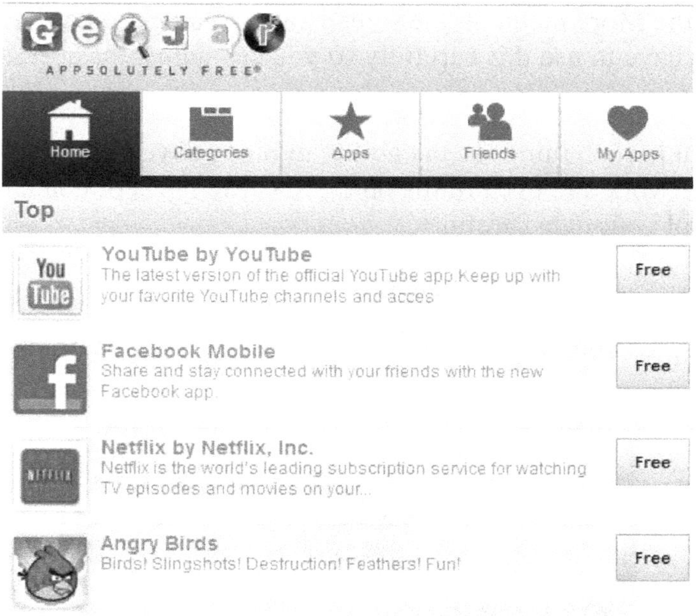

1. Log onto a website that lists these applications. You can use the GetJar website as one option, for instance.
2. Click on the appropriate installation link for a particular app. Most of these apps should be free to use because they are not going to be linked up to the Amazon Kindle network.
3. Be sure to check on each individual application on a site like this. You have to make sure that each app is reviewed to see if it is actually safe to use. The problem with third party apps is that they tend to be dangerous because they have not been endorsed by Google, the company that operates the Android operating system that the Kindle family of products uses.

This could be used to download some applications that are normally used on the Apple iPad or other kinds of devices. Could you even imagine reading the Barnes and Noble Nook program on the Kindle Fire? You could do this if you use the right method for getting different kinds of articles on your site.

Chapter 13 – Parental Controls

The Kindle Fire and Kindle Fire HD are both made with a series of convenient parental controls. You can use them by opening the More menu on the screen and by using the Parental Controls section to adjust these settings. You have to use this carefully so you can adjust the access that your kids might get to the device.

The parental controls include such things as the ability to block a web browser and emails, the ability to block access to a Wi-Fi network and even limits on the specific types of content that your kids can access. You have to control your data carefully.

93. Creating a Password

While you can get a good password set up on your Kindle Fire, you have to do a few things with parental controls in mind.

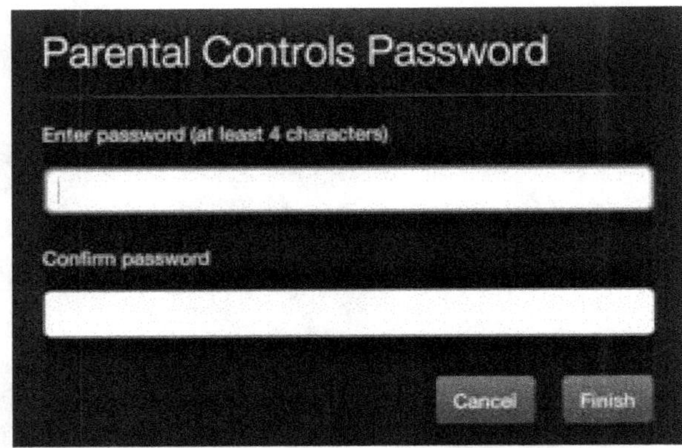

1. Go to the Parental Controls section of the reader and use the password option.
2. Create a password that is different from the password used on the rest of the Kindle Fire.
3. Make sure you avoid using a password that is very easy to guess or figure out.

94. Creating Daily Limits

You can adjust the Kindle Fire by using a series of time limits relating to how long a child can use the Kindle Fire for during the course of a certain time.

1. Control the total screen time for the first part of the process. You should do this before adjusting the other items to make sure that you create a general limit on what can be done here.
2. Adjust the content activity time based on how long you want your kids to use things on the Kindle Fire. For example, you can allow your kids to read books as long as they want but also limit application use to about thirty to sixty minutes.

95. Control Specific Apps

There are several things to do when it comes to adjusting your kids' access to applications. While you could hide your apps from them, the best thing to do is to restrict the ways how they can use these apps at times. Here's what you can do in this case.

1. Go to the Manage Content section of the parental controls section of the reader.
2. Select individual items in the book, video and application categories.
3. Add check marks to whatever items it is you want your kids to actually access. Leave any boxes that contain objectionable materials clear so your kids will not get access to any particular spot.

96. Controlling Your Main Display

You can use a few controls on your Kindle Fire to keep the main display of your device safe for your kids to use.

1. Remove objectionable items from your Carousel before giving it to your kids. You can do this by holding down on an item on the Carousel and then choosing the delete the item from that spot.
2. Limit access to the cloud if possible. The parental controls section will remove the cloud sections so your kids will not try to get in there.
3. Prepare a special display by using the Freetime application. This feature on newer versions of the Kindle Fire can be used to change the information listed on the Kindle Fire by focusing on family-friendly applications and media files. You can adjust the items that will be accessible on this part of the display by using this feature on the reader.

97. Adding an Additional Application

You can use a few other applications on your reader to make it easier for your reader to stay intact. These go beyond the Freetime app you might already use on the Kindle Fire.

1. Download an application like the Kids Place with Child Lock application. This could be used with a lock feature that restarts the reader in the event that a child goes out of the range of protection on the reader.
2. Use an application for blocking marketplace purchases or access. The Kid Mode Play and Learn application is a good choice to use in this case.
3. Be sure that you use an application that adds passwords to individual applications. The Smart App Protector is an application to take a look at.

98. Using the Smart App Protector

The Smart App Protector is a popular application to use when maintaining your reader by keeping kids from accessing different application. Here is a look at how you can use this.

1. Download the Smart App Protector for your Kindle Fire or Kindle Fire HD.
2. Open the app and add passwords for all your applications. You should use different passwords for each individual application. Just be sure that you keep your passwords written down in a secure spot where your kids are not likely to access that paper.
3. Use the appropriate finger motion to open access to the entry box for applying the password as needed. This finger motion feature is used to add to the protection that comes with the application by adding a layer of control.
4. The password entry box should open when the right motion is used. You can enter in the appropriate password in this spot.
5. You can turn off this protective measure by going back to the protector and disabling it as needed.

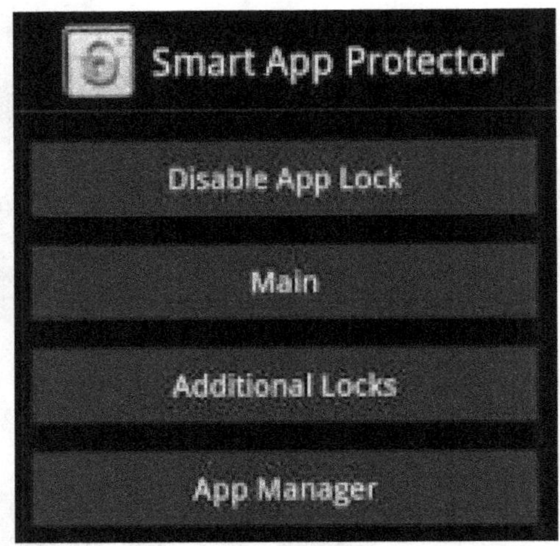

The adjustments that you make on the reader should be used on all of the applications you have. Check on this to make sure that you lock onto the proper apps that you want to keep people from reading.

Chapter 14 – Display and Photo Ideas

99. How to Access the Camera

While it is true that the Kindle Fire HD supports the use of a camera, it is very difficult to actually get it to take pictures. However, you can find the hidden camera application on the Kindle Fire HD by using these steps.

1. Download the ES File Explorer program. You should be able to find it through the Kindle App Store.
2. Open the program as soon as you download it.
3. Got to the AppMgr button on the screen.
4. Touch the Category menu and click on the Systems Apps section.
5. This will then list the details on the many different applications you can use. You should be able to find a Camera app at this point. Click on that to open the application.

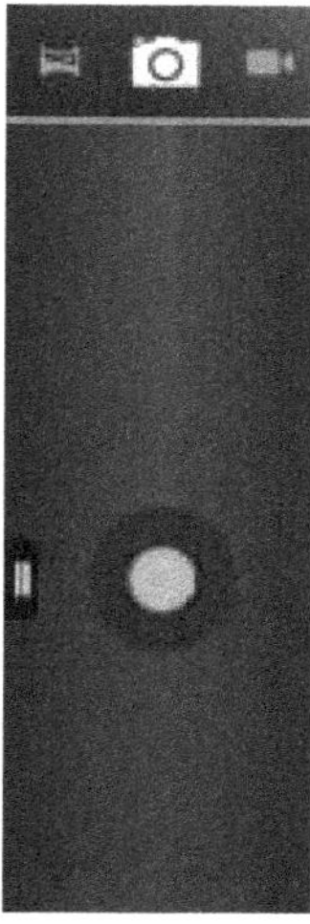

6. You can then take a picture with the camera. You can touch the blue button as it appears.

You will have to turn the Kindle around if you want to do this. There is no camera on the back end of the Kindle. There is only one on the front. It is used primarily with video conferencing and Skype support in mind.

100. How to View Photos

Your photos can be seen by opening them up through any photo-viewing program on your Kindle. Here is how you can do this:

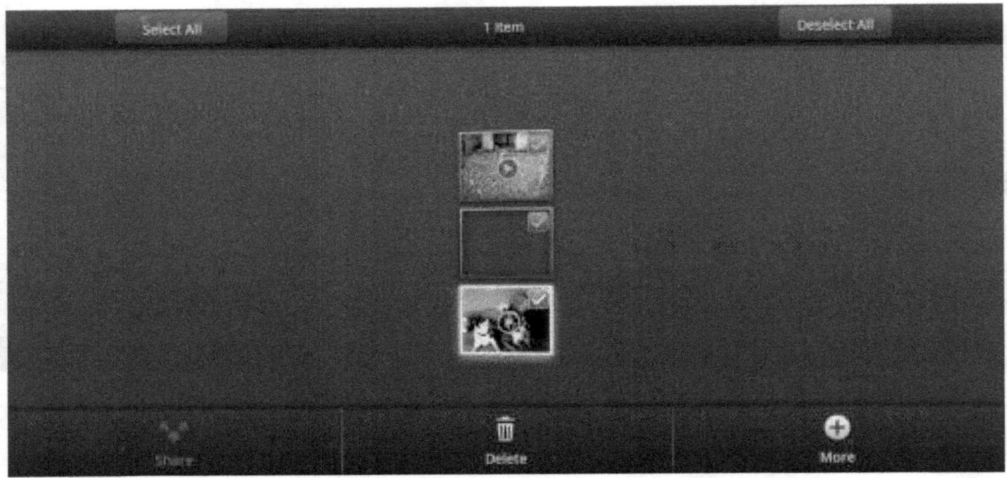

1. Go to the Gallery section of your reader.
2. Tap the Pictures section to find an appropriate item to view.
3. You can also tap the Slideshow option to view all of your pictures in a slideshow format.

101. How to Shoot Videos

This procedure is dedicated to using the video camera feature on the Kindle Fire or Kindle Fire HD.

1. Open the same Camera application through what you did on the last page.
2. Touch the small image that looks like a video camera. It should be to the right of the traditional camera photo.

This should appear on the same place that you took a photo in.

3. Touch the blue button as seen earlier to start recording a video.
4. Touch the button again when you are done recording.
5. You can also adjust the image settings and sound recording features but this is all up to your discretion.

The videos that you shoot should now be accessible through a standard video player on your reader.

102. How to Resize Photos

You will have to go online to resize photos on your reader. This procedure is used to help you out with adjusting pictures the way you see fit. You can do this by cropping or resizing pictures.

1. Choose the photo you want to resize.

2. Go to Pixlr.com on your Kindle web browser. You can also download the Pixlr application from this site.

3. Click on the Resize or Crop icon on the settings. These are found on the far left end of the control bar.

4. The file should then be adjusted based on the number of pixels you want to use or which sections you want to trim off from the edges.

5. The picture file can then be saved in the format you want it to be saved in. This should work well if you want to reduce the size of your photo.

103. How to Edit Pictures

You can also edit pictures with the same program.

1. Go to the Pixlr website or use the Pixlr application.

2. Check your photo for blur, red eye or contrast issues.

3. Use the individual icons to adjust your picture as you see fit.

4. You may also use the Auto Fix option to change the photo with settings based on what the application or website feels is best for your page.

104. How to Remove Items From the Kindle Carousel

Sometimes you might not use certain items on your Kindle for a while but they are still on your Carousel anyway. You can clear out this clutter and shorten the size of the Carousel with this process.

1. Tap the appropriate icon on your Kindle Carousel. Hold your finger on it.

2. You should then choose the option to remove the item from the Carousel.

3. The Carousel will now be cleared out. The item will return the next time you open it.

This process works best if you have the most recent edition of the Kindle Fire software installed. The newest versions of the program tend to work the best.

105. How to Email Photos on Your Kindle to Other People

1. Open an album in your Photos library. This should include both the files you have saved onto your Kindle Fire and the photos you have taken with your Kindle Fire HD.
2. Touch the icon that looks like an envelope.

3. Choose the email account you will be sending the photo from. This will be your Kindle Fire HD account by default.
4. Select the photo or photos you want to send out.
5. Choose the destination email address.
6. Tap the Send Photos button to send the photos by email.

106. Import Facebook Photos

You can move photos from Facebook onto your Kindle Fire. Here's how you can do this.

1. Connect your Kindle Fire to an appropriate Facebook account.

2. Click on the Import button on the control panel in your photo gallery. This button should have the Facebook logo right next to it.
3. Your Facebook photos should then be moved onto your cloud drive.
4. You will have to move all your Facebook photos onto the cloud. There are no features at this time that will allow you to select only a few photos from a Facebook account.
5. You can then add new photos as needed by touching the same Import button again if you ever get any new photos to move onto your Kindle.

107. How to Rename Photo Albums

You can rename your photo albums so you can have an easier time organizing your photos and viewing them based on the specific things that you want to find. Here's a look at how you rename them.

1. Press and hold the specific album name that you want to change.
2. Touch the Rename display as it comes up.
3. Enter in the new photo album name with the virtual keyboard.

4. The new name should be displayed on your Kindle and on your cloud account.

108. Adjusting the Wallpaper

Amazon already uses standard wallpaper for creating unique images but you can easily adjust the wallpaper to feature your own particular images. Here are a few steps relating to how you can create rotating wallpaper that uses multiple images that can switch on occasion.

1. Download the Rotating Wallpaper app for your Kindle. This should be free to install.

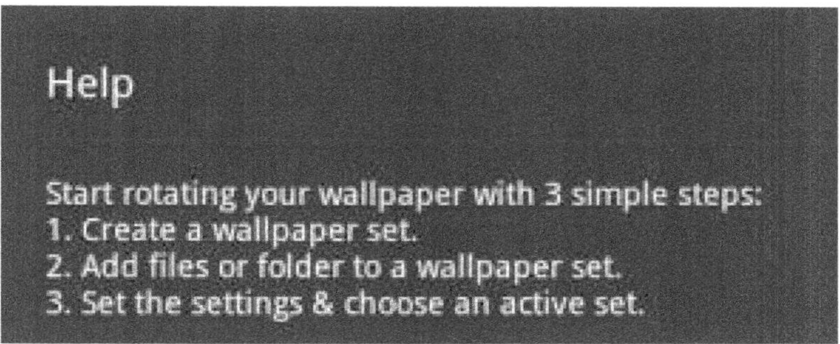

2. You can then access the program by creating a wallpaper set. You can click on the Add Set button at the bottom left of the application.
3. Enter the name of the set you will be using.
4. Add the picture files from your Kindle into the set.
5. The settings can then be adjusted. These will be controlled based on the timing that the wallpaper will move around on, the way how a picture fits the screen and even the order that the photos can appear in.
6. The wallpaper will now change every few hours based on your discretion.

109. How to Take Screenshots

You can take screenshots of what's on your Kindle with ease depending on the model that you are using. The process is clearly easier to use on the HD version of the tablet than it is for the older standard version.

The Kindle Fire HD requires you to do the following to take a screenshot:

1. Press the power and volume down buttons at the same time.
2. The photo will then be on the Photos section of your reader. This should be found in the Screenshots folder.

The standard Kindle Fire has a much more complicated process to use when finding your photos. It takes a while to do it but this process can be done if you use an appropriate system for getting images captured off of the reader.

1. Install the Android SDK onto your Kindle Fire. Go to developer.android.com to access this part of your device.

2. Connect your Kindle to your computer with a USB drive. The SDK can be uploaded to the Kindle from there.

3. Go to the CD Tools section of your SDK directory after you install the SDK into an appropriate folder based on your preference.

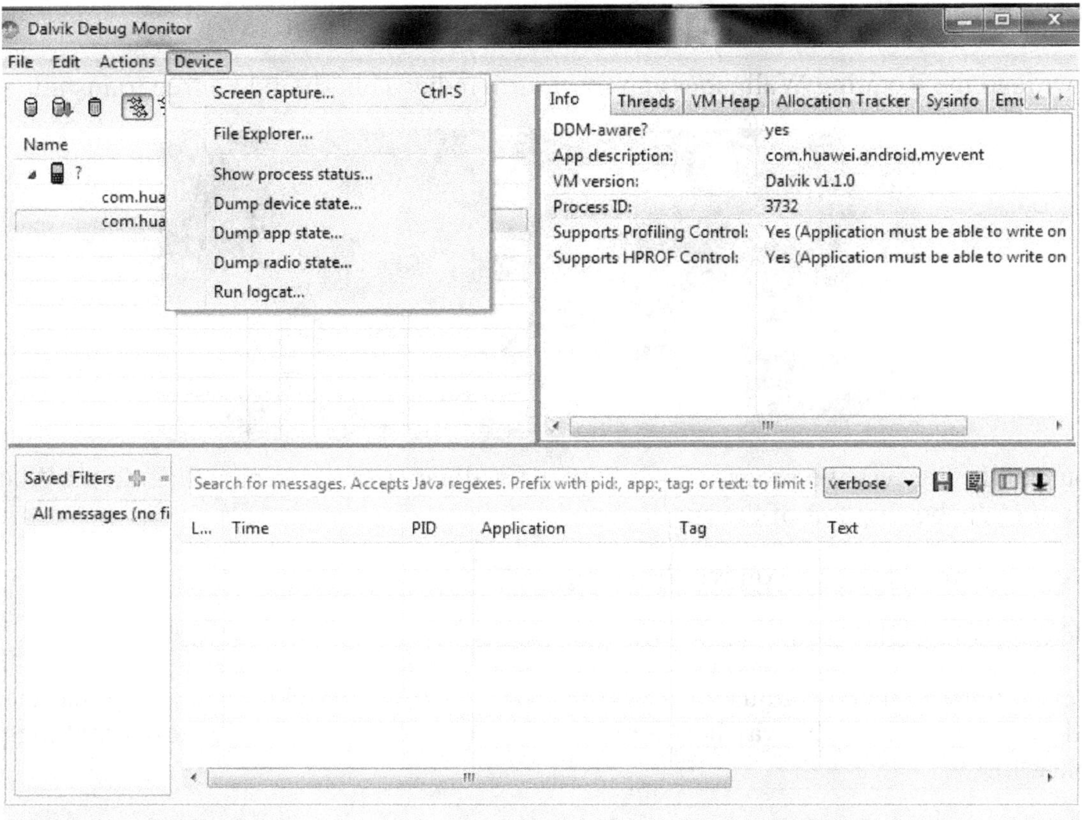

4. Type in **ddms** to run the Dalvick Debug Monitor. This is a debug tool that should be found in the reader.

5. Use the Device menu on the screen and click on the Screen Capture button. This should be done as you have moved the Kindle onto a particular screen that you want to take a picture of.

6. The image will be taken and saved onto your Kindle as a PNG file.

No matter which device you use, you have to be aware that **the Kindle Fire will not allow you to take screenshots of any video files that you play back. Any video screenshots will come up as black boxes.** This is done as a means of securing video files so they cannot be easily copied.

110. How to Change the Interface

While it is true that the Kindle Fire and Kindle Fire HD both use an easy to maintain and run interface, you might benefit off of a different interface if you use something else. This is made with an easy to use series of steps.

This could be used with many different interface options. We'll use the Go Launcher EX option for this example. It is the most popular choice among all the different solutions anyone can get.

1. Download the Go Launcher EX application.
2. Tap the appropriate button to install the program as soon as you are done getting it.
3. You will then have the ability to use the Go Launcher EX program as your main user interface. You can get into this by restarting your Kindle Fire and by then selecting the particular interface you want. Select the Go Launcher EX option and choose the box that makes this the default selection.
4. You will now have access to the Go Launcher EX interface. This will allow you to customize the interface of your Kindle Fire in any way that you see fit.

Think of this as a way how you can get your very own special display set up on your reader. It might make it look a little closer to a traditional tablet.

Remember, this is going to be used as the default interface after you install it and choose it for your needs. However, you can go back to the old interface if desired later on.

111. How to Revert Your Interface

You can go back to the old Kindle Fire interface in the event that you feel that your modified interface is not all that interesting to you or you simply want to go back to the old one that you used to have.

1. Go to the settings section of the new interface you are using.
2. Choose the application option in this section.
3. Go through the different settings you have with regards to what programs are the defaults and what are not.
4. Select the interface setting that you are using and remove the default option from the interface.
5. Restart the Kindle Fire or shut it down and start it back up again. The device should then ask you what interface you want to use at the start. You can choose to take in the old Kindle Fire interface and use that as the default once again.

You can always uninstall the new interface option you selected as soon as you are done reverting back to the Kindle Fire default. This new interface option will still be accessible on your cloud account for later use if you want to get back on it later on.

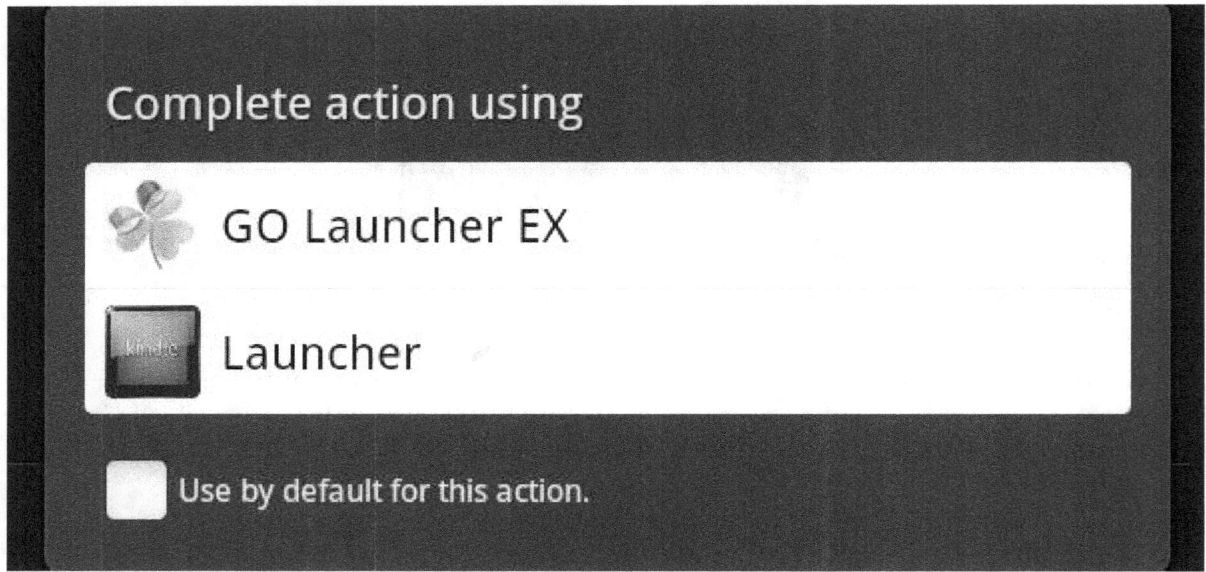

Chapter 15 – Online Tips and Tricks

You can go online once you are able to get the Wi-Fi connection to your Kindle Fire HD set up. Here are some online tips and tricks that will give you the most out of your reader.

112. Clearing Your Cache

Your Kindle Fire will develop a cache featuring a series of old Silk browser files after a while. This can not only take up more space on your hard drive but also cause the reader to slow down after a while. You can clear these unnecessary files by using this process.

1. Go to the Settings section of your Silk browser.
2. Go to the Clear All Cookie Data option.
3. Choose the Clear Cache option. The old cache files should be removed.

113. Clear Your Browsing History

Your browser history can also take up hard drive space and slow your Kindle down. You can clear in out with this process.

1. Go to the Settings menu in the browser.
2. Go into the same Clear All Cookie Data section that you used when clearing out the cache files.
3. Choose the Clear History option.

114. Block Pop-Ups

The Kindle Fire HD is not immune to pop-up adverts. Fortunately, you can keep them from showing up on your browser when you use these steps.

1. Access the Settings menu in the Silk browser.
2. Go to the Block Pop-Up Windows section.
3. Choose the appropriate setting when you enter this section. You should choose Always so every single pop-up will be blocked.
4. You can also choose to let the Kindle Fire accept pop-ups on a by request basis. You can choose the appropriate option in this part of the menu. This may be useful if you have to get access to a specific pop-up at a given time. Otherwise, the Always option will be good enough

115. Changing Your Default Search Engine

You can adjust the reader based on the search engine that you prefer to use. This is perfect for cases where you just want to type in a keyword into the URL box and get results off of that keyword. You can do this with the following process.

1. Use the Settings menu in your Silk browser.
2. Choose the Set Search Engine option.
3. You will have access to one of many different search engines. Google is generally the basic default but you can also use Yahoo or Bing according to your general preference.

116. How to Search for Items Quickly

It might be easy for you to search for items on your Kindle Fire without having to go a search engine's website to load it up first. Here is a look at what you have to do in order to get into this feature.

1. Enter in a keyword into the URL bar at the top of the screen.
2. Wait for the default search engine you have set up to display the appropriate results.
3. Tap the proper result that you want to search for.
4. The browser will redirect you to the search results for the specific keyword that you have entered into the reader.

This can be used on your search engine no matter what particular search engine you want to use in this process.

117. How to Switch to Desktop Display

Sometimes a website might not be able to read on your browser in its mobile form. This is a real hassle for some sites but that does not mean that you have to stick with the mobile version of a site every single time you use your Kindle Fire. Here's a process for correcting this issue.

1. Enter in the URL of whatever site you are trying to access.
2. Tap the space in your URL.
3. Replace the "m" at the beginning of the display with a "www" to use the desktop edition instead of the mobile edition
4. The general browser version of the site should load up instead of the mobile version.

118. How to Change the Default Display

You can also change the default display on your Kindle Fire browser to make it so the reader will always display the desktop version of a site.

1. Go to the Settings menu.
2. Go to the Requested Website View part of the General section of the menu.
3. Choose between the Desktop or Mobile option. You can also choose the Automatic version to let it move into whatever version is default for your site.

Chapter 16 – Fixing Problems

There is always the risk that your Kindle Fire might run into a few problems here and there. There are a number of useful tips that you can use to keep your Kindle Fire from being more of a hassle than it has to be.

119. Getting an Amazon Account

One of the biggest issues people have when using the Kindle Fire is that they aren't using them with appropriate Amazon accounts. You clearly have to use an Amazon account if you want your reader to be useful. You can fix this problem with the following steps.

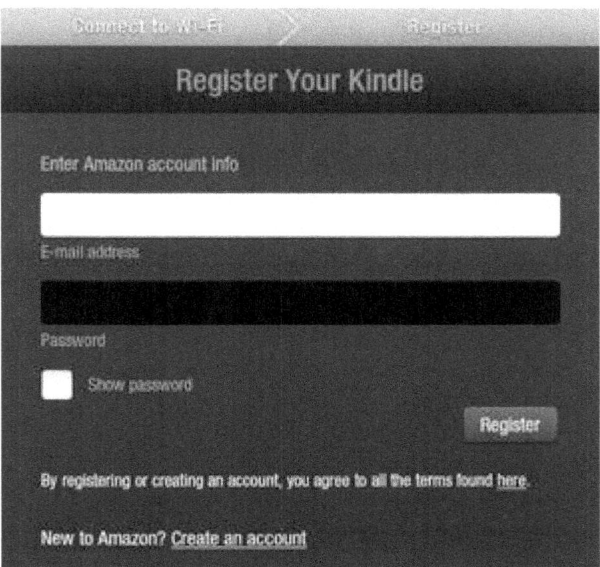

1. Go to the More section of the menu on the top of the Kindle Fire.
2. Tap the My Account button.
3. Use the Create an Account link to set up your own account.
4. You will have to set up your own username, password and credit card payment information alongside some other points to set up your account.

120. Resetting a Password

Sometimes you might have to reset the password on your Kindle Fire in the event that the data on your Kindle has been compromised. Be aware that **this will delete the content on your Kindle Fire but you can reinstall all that content after you register your device again.**

1. Go to the More spot on the menu.
2. Choose the Device section.
3. Choose the Reset to Factory Defaults option to reset the data on your reader.
4. Register the Kindle Fire again with your name and with a new password.

Remember, the password that you can use on your Kindle Fire is going to be different from what you might use for your Amazon.com account. It is best to keep both of these passwords different from each other to protect the data on your reader so it will not get into any trouble.

121. Fixing a Frozen Screen

The screen on your Kindle Fire can freeze up after a while. This might come from a lack of an appropriate battery charge to keep it running right. In other cases this will come from your Kindle Fire not being able to download files properly or even programs that are not responding to your needs properly. You will have to do the following the correct this problem.

1. Hold the power button on your device for about fifteen to twenty seconds.
2. The device should turn off after this time.
3. Press the button again to start the reader back up.

122. Updating Your System

You may need to update your system so it can keep on running as well as possible. This should be used to give your reader access to the latest software. In fact, you might even have more protective for your system if you use the latest version of the device's software.

Kindle Software Updates

Select your Kindle to see the latest available software updates.

Kindle Fire HD 8.9"

Kindle Fire HD 7"

Kindle Fire (2nd Generation)

Kindle Fire (1st Generation)

Kindle Paperwhite

Kindle

Kindle Touch

Kindle Keyboard

1. Go to the Amazon Kindle update website at amazon.com/kindlesoftwareupdates.
2. Choose the appropriate Kindle model that you want to update.
3. Connect your Kindle Fire to your computer by a USB drive and install the appropriate software update directly onto your computer.
4. Move the file you downloaded to the kindleupdates folder on your Kindle Fire. You should be able to do this because your reader will interpret your Kindle Fire as an external hard drive when you plug it into your computer.
5. Open the file on your reader as soon as it moves over to your drive.
6. The file should install itself onto your reader. It will also ask your reader to restart so it will read the newest edition of the Kindle software.

123. Showing a Password

The Kindle Fire will automatically censor passwords as they are entered into the reader. This is used to protect your data from other people. However, you can also fix this by having all the characters in your password be displayed as you are entering it in. This might be convenient for you because it is not like other people might peek over your back when you are entering this data in.

This has to be used well among all tips and tricks for the device because there is a real chance that you might be forced to format your reader if you use the wrong password. The Kindle Fire will reset if you fail to use the right password to log into it after four attempts for using it.

1. Tap the Show Password box need to the entry form.

2. Type in your password. You should be able to see all its characters as you enter them.
3. Tap the box again when you are done. This is to make sure the option is turned off the next time the device is opened.

124. Getting the USB Port to Read

Sometimes your computer might not actually read your Kindle Fire or Kindle Fire HD after you link it up. Your computer might display an error message or it will simply not show up as an external hard drive.

Either way, you have to use these tips to get the Kindle Fire to actually be read by the computer.

1. Restart the Kindle Fire before plugging it back in.
2. Try using a different USB port on a computer. For example, a port on the back side of your computer is often more likely to work than one on the front.
3. Restart your computer after you connect the Kindle Fire to it. Be sure that the reader is on while you are doing this.

The computer should read your device after it loads back up. You may want to check your computer's explorer menu to see if the reader is showing up as an external hard drive just like if you placed a memory card or flash drive in that slot.

125. Deregistering a Kindle Fire

You may choose to deregister your Kindle Fire in the event that you are going to replace it with a new model or if you want to give it as a gift to someone. You can do this with one of two options:

1. Go to the More section of the settings on the top of the reader.
2. Go to the My Account section.
3. Choose the Deregister option to remove your name and account from the reader.
4. The reader will then ask you to enter in a new name to register the account with.
5. You can also use an alternate option by going to the Manage Your Kindle website on a computer and by clicking on the Deregister link on the Manage Your Devices section of this site.

126. Cleaning the Screen

The Kindle Fire, like many other tablets, tends to develop smears after a while. This is from all the activity used on the tablet to keep it working properly. You can clean off the screen to make it look good as new while also improving your ability to see it in the dark.

Just be careful when you are using this because it can be a real challenge to utilize the cleaning process with the wrong materials.

1. Make sure you use a soft white cloth to clean off the screen. Do not use anything rough because it might scratch or screen or leave a bunch of fibers all over the screen. You could particularly use a soft pad made specifically for wiping off the touch screen if you wish to use one.

2. Add a small bit of water to the tip of a cloth and use that on the screen. You can pat it down and dry it with the same patting motion to keep it under control. This is useful provided that you are not too fast with it.

3. Avoid using any glass cleaner as you are doing this. Although the Kindle Fire does have a screen that is made of glass, you should avoid glass cleaner because it can damage the components. Also, there is a potential that you will get lots of streaking marks on the screen if you use a glass cleaner to take care of it.

127. Cleaning the Headphone Jack

The small headphone jack on your Kindle Fire can develop some junk in it after a while. You can clean this out if you use the right materials for doing so.

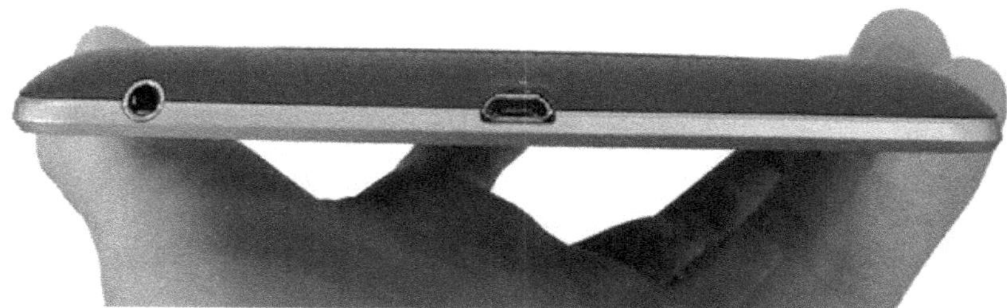

Although you can hold onto the Kindle Fire while using these procedures, you may want to lay it on a flat surface where it will not shift as you are working on it.

1. Use an air can to blow the area inside the jack. This is to remove dust, lint and other items that might get in the way of the jack.

2. A dry cotton swab can also be added and waved into the area after using an air can. This can be done to gather some of the loose materials inside the headphone jack. Be extremely gentle during this step and do not try to rub it too hard on any surface or you will risk creating damages.

3. A small piece of tape can also be wired around a paper clip with the sticky side facing outwards. You can do this if you are careful enough and the clip does not puncture or adhere to any spots in the headphone jack.

These are all used to make sure your headphones can actually fit into the jack. This is also so the headphones will be clearly read by the jack. Don't forget to check the headphones yourself to see if they are working properly and if they are using the right wires for keeping them intact.

128. Controlling Audio Books

The problem with some players is that they fail to read their audio books the right way. This is often due to an improper file format being used in the process. You can fix this problem by doing the following when reading your book.

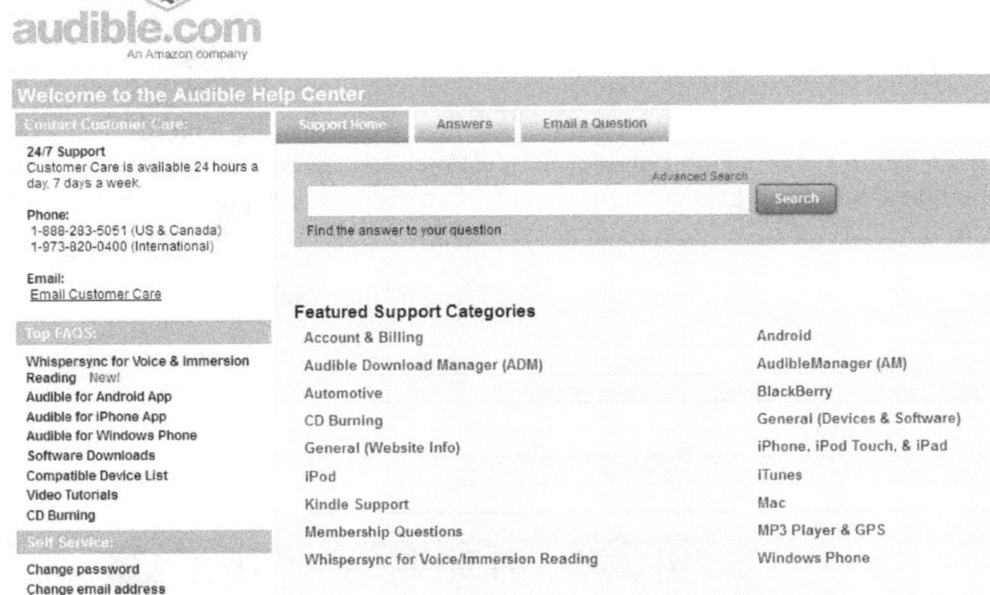

1. Attach your reader to a USB cable and link it up to your computer.
2. Go to the Audible folder on your Kindle Fire. This is where your audio book files should be.
3. Check on the files to see if they are .aa or .aax files.
4. Contact Audible at audible.custhelp.com in the event that you are experiencing an issue with a file. Audible should provide you with a free download of the file in a correct format.

129. Fixing Document Issues

Sometimes the documents that you can download or read on your Kindle Fire or Kindle Fire HD might not run as well as it should. This is often due to an issue relating to your file not running well. You have to use the right procedure to get a particular file to be read on your reader.

1. Confirm that the person who is sending a document to your reader is an authorized email on your Manage Your Kindle menu.
2. Link your reader up to a computer in an attempt to get it to link up properly.
3. Sync the Kindle Fire by touching the Sync button on the top of the unit.
4. Go to the Your Pending Deliveries section of the Manage Your Kindle page to see if the document you are trying to get is available.

Chapter 17 – Virus Protection

Even portable devices can be susceptible to viruses. There is always the risk that your reader could be impacted by a virus from a malicious website.

It is clearly best for you to avoid going to any website that might be questionable in nature. This includes websites that are not protected or websites that appear to feature unusual content. However, there are a few other tips and tricks that need to be used so you can protect your device.

130. Download an Antivirus Program to Your Computer

You should consider downloading an antivirus program onto your computer so you can link your Kindle Fire up to it and then have it read the data on there. Here's how you can do this.

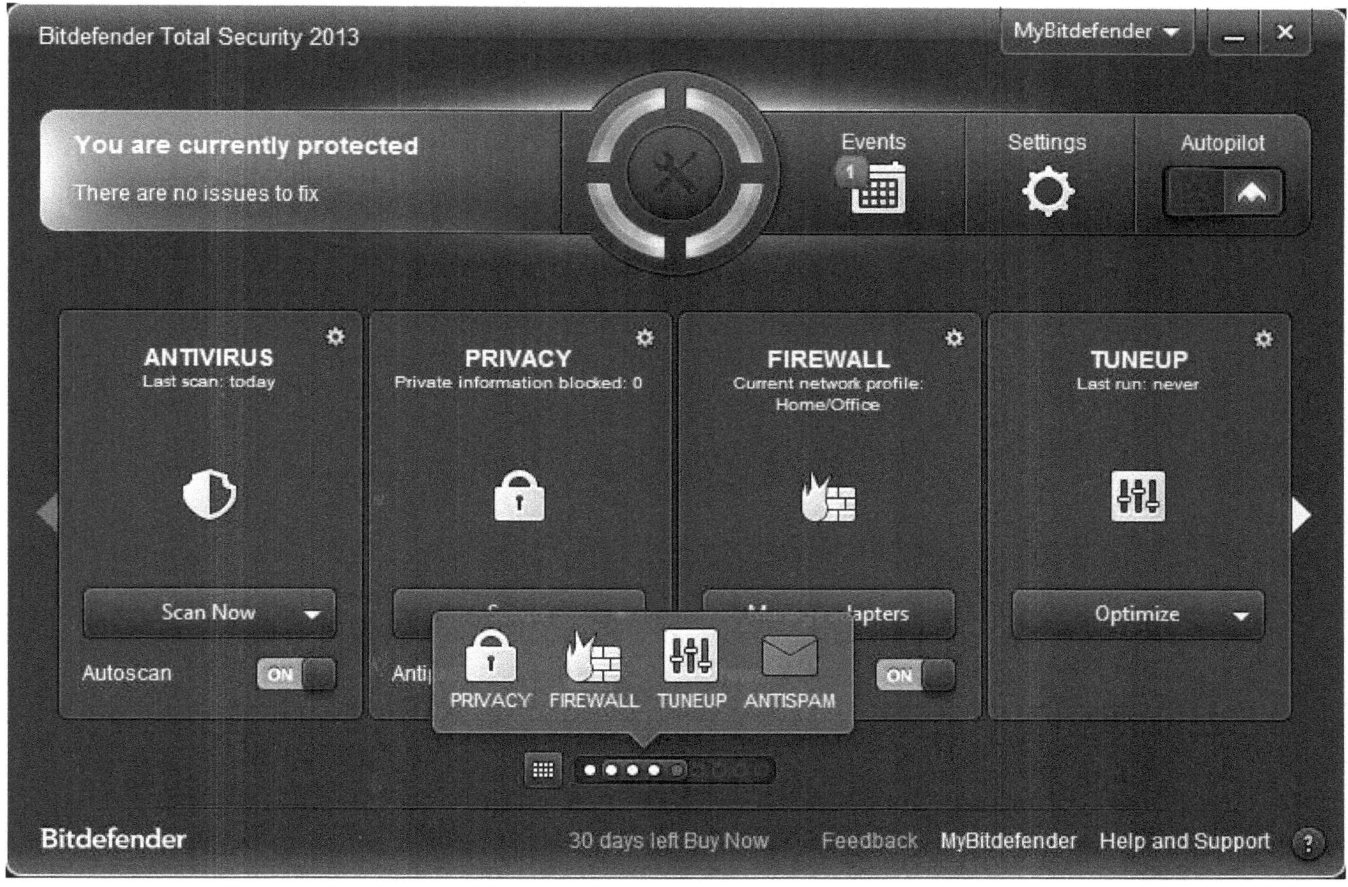

1. Download a program that is suitable for Kindle Fire use. The BitDefender 2013 Total Security program is the option featured in the picture right above this tip.
2. Connect your reader to a computer that has this program.
3. Use the scanning feature to check on your reader. It should access your reader by checking on it as an external hard drive.
4. The program should also clean up any viruses or other problems that it might find.
5. Unhook the Kindle Fire from your computer as soon as the scanning and cleaning procedures are done. Do not remove it from the computer while the scan is in progress or else it could end up causing damages to the device's file system.

131. Download an Application

The next choice for you to use will involve downloading an application onto your Kindle Fire.

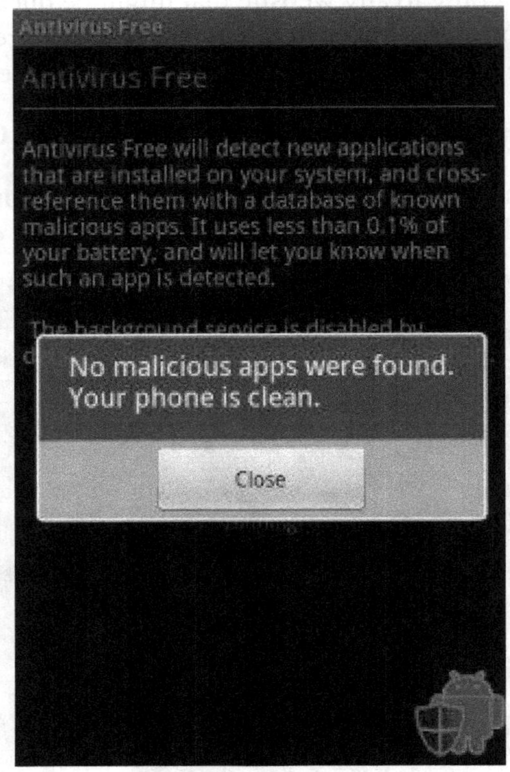

1. Go to the application store and search for an appropriate option.
2. Download the app and run it from your unit. Creative's Antivirus Free is the example that we will use in this step. A picture of the program is attached to this particular tip.
3. Use the program to check and see if the Kindle is running properly. You can start by touching an appropriate scanning button to check all the files on the reader.
4. The device will spend a few minutes looking through your reader to check for harmful files.
5. You can also update the program on occasion to make sure it reads the latest virus definitions. The updating feature can be easy to find on an average program. For example, the Antivirus Free program uses this feature on the Settings section.

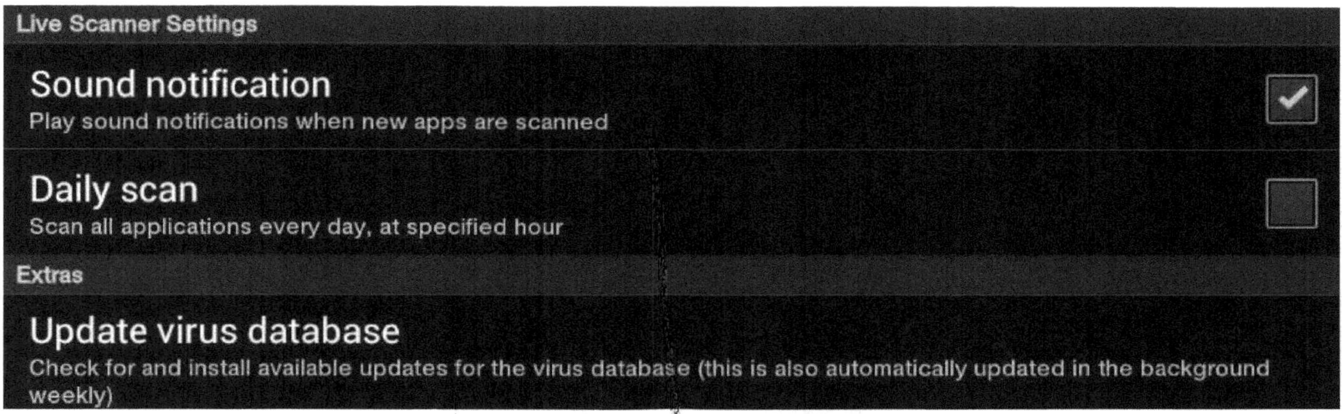

132. Use a Daily Scan

An antivirus program can also be used to adjust the daily scans on your device. This is used provided that the reader is on during the time when the scan is to take place.

1. Open your antivirus program and go to its settings menu.
2. Set details on when a daily scan is to occur.
3. Set the specific hour that you want to use this scan on.
4. Leave the reader on when the time for the scan occurs. The program will not scan your reader if it is not on at the appropriate time.

133. Firewall Support

A firewall can be used to protect your reader from serious problems that relate to other people trying to break into your device and read its contents. This is particularly important for cases where you are on a public network that can be accessed by anyone without a password.

1. Make sure you get your Kindle Fire to take in third party applications before you use this process. Refer to the earlier tip in this guide for additional information on sideloading.
2. Use the new support to install a firewall program like DroidWall. This is a free application used to limit the apps on your device that can access a network.

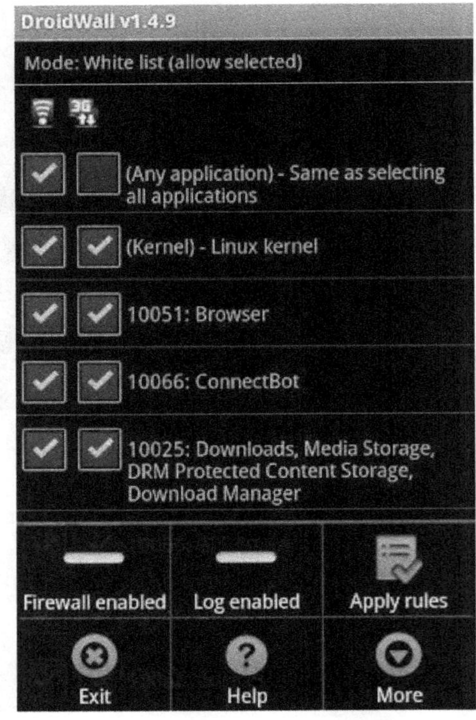

3. Adjust the program by using a section to apply rules for what programs can go online.
4. You can disable the firewall when you get out of a public network and back into a private one. The firewall may be protective but it can also use up more battery space than what you could afford to use at a given time.

Chapter 18 – Bluetooth Support

You can use a Bluetooth connection to link your Kindle Fire HD up to a number of different devices that also have Bluetooth support. However, this does not work on the standard Kindle Fire. However, you can change that with a particular adapter to keep your signals running right.

This is the Bluetooth logo. This should state when the system is active on your reader. This appears on the Kindle Fire HD but you can also find this on devices that any Kindle Fire model could link up to if you have the right adapter or connection going.

134. Add a Bluetooth Adapter

A Bluetooth adapter can be placed on your Kindle Fire to give it the support it needs so you can use it with all sorts of Bluetooth devices. This is not required for use on a Kindle Fire HD but the support for the standard Kindle Fire will certainly be worth it.

1. Attach an appropriate adapter through the headphone jack in the Kindle Fire.
2. Turn the adapter on as needed.
3. Keep the adapter located near an appropriate Bluetooth signal. While the adapter can add to the functionality of the reader, a typical adapter is only going to work at distances of ten to thirty feet on average. You will have to stay close to the area you want to use in order to get this to work properly.

135. Connecting Devices

The process for connecting a device onto your Kindle Fire HD is easy to follow. These steps are made to help you not only find Bluetooth devices but also get them linked up to your reader in real time.

1. Turn on the Bluetooth-enabled device that you want to link up to.
2. Tap the Wireless menu on the top of the screen.
3. Tap the Bluetooth option and then enable the system.
4. Check the Available Devices section to see what devices are available for you to use. This should be used with any device that has been activated for use.

136. Using a Bluetooth Keyboard

A Bluetooth keyboard can add to the functionality of the Kindle Fire. This will give you a full-size keyboard that you can use without having to add any wires going to the Kindle. You can use this by following these steps.

1. Turn on the Bluetooth keyboard if it has an applicable switch. It should also run with a few batteries.
2. Place the keyboard right in front of the screen. You should use a cover with a stand on your reader so it can prop itself up to look like its own computer monitor. This will be displayed in a landscape format.
3. Connect the keyboard to your reader through either the Bluetooth menu or through the Bluetooth adapter on the reader depending on your model.
4. The keyboard should be ready to use whenever you touch the screen and reach a data entry spot that the keyboard can be used in.

The best part of this is that the Bluetooth keyboard will be made to work a little easier than what you'd get out of the Kindle Fire keyboard. While the keyboard on the reader itself is convenient, the Bluetooth keyboard will be even better because it works exactly like what you'd expect to find on a regular computer.

Just be sure that the keyboard actually has Bluetooth support. Not all keyboards are made to use this feature. Some only link up wirelessly with very specific models.

137. Controlling Bluetooth Interference

Sometimes other signals can get in the way of your Bluetooth device and cause interference issues to occur. This is a real burden because it often keeps your Kindle Fire from linking up with another object.

The fact is that the Bluetooth signals you get operate under the same 2.4 GHz 802.11b band that some other wireless devices work with. Therefore, your signals may get lost in the process.

You may need to do the following to keep this interference under control:

1. Move your wireless items around in your space to where the risk of Bluetooth signals being disrupted will be minimized.
2. Adjust the wireless items in your area by controlling their wireless systems. You might need to use adapters on these items to get them to support a larger 5 GHz bandwidth. This bandwidth will not get in the way of your Bluetooth devices.
3. Turn off any wireless items that might get in the way of your Bluetooth connection. You might need to do this in order to protect the quality of your connection.
4. Try and move the Bluetooth interface closer to your reader. Sometimes this might be used to minimize the physical space between the items and therefore reduce the potential for your signals to become lost in the process. Of course, you will have to be careful when setting this because all of your items will have an extremely limited range.

It should not be too difficult for you to fix the problems relating to interference on your Bluetooth connection. You should have access to your Bluetooth signals secured if you use the right procedures.

Chapter 19 – Microphone Use

You can add a microphone to your Kindle Fire for all sorts of purposes. You can use a microphone on your unit for just a few dollars depending on the model that you have and the type of microphone you buy for it.

138. Setting Up a Microphone

You can quickly set up a microphone to use on your reader. Here is a step by step process for how you can do this.

1. Buy an appropriate microphone with headset product that uses a 3.5mm jack.

2. Check on the connections used on your microphone. It has to use a 4-connector TRRS plug in order to work properly.
3. Plug the device into the 3.5mm jack on the side of the reader.
4. Test your microphone with an appropriate recording program. We'll get into using these programs in just a bit.
5. You will have to use a set that includes a small series of headphones attached to it. These headphones are to be used so you can hear what you are saying after things are recorded.

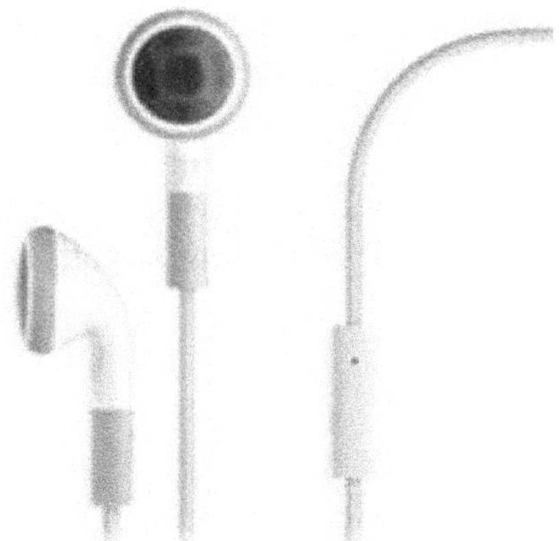

A basic model should include standard ear buds.

139. Finding a Microphone App

You'll have to sideload a microphone app onto your Kindle Fire because the device does not support microphones in its basic form.

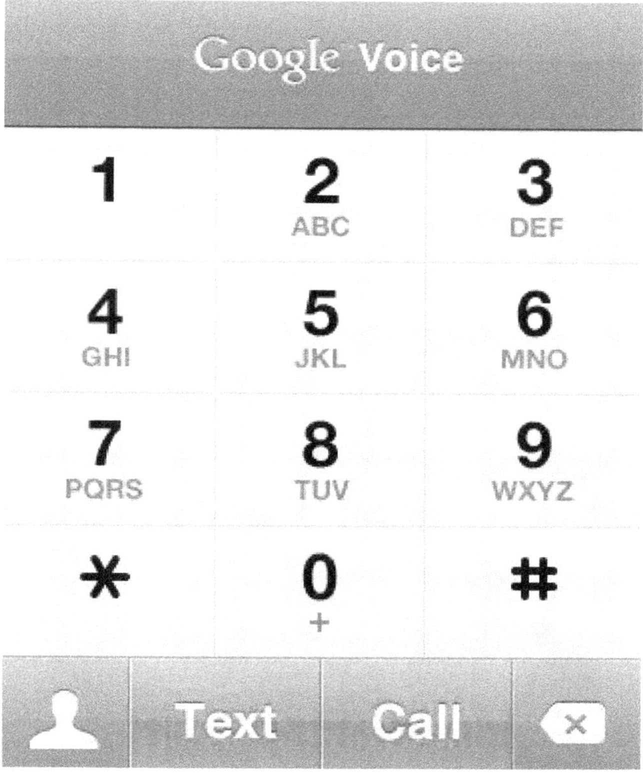

1. Follow the appropriate instructions listed earlier in this guide on how to find an appropriate third party application.

2. Download a program used to record your voice with. Google Voice should be good enough.

The program you use should be designed to simply record your voice or to allow other people to hear it over another network. The features on an application will vary based on the specific kind of application you are using so be sure to compare your options with each other.

140. Record Audio

You can record audio for all kinds of purposes on your Kindle Fire or Kindle Fire HD. You have to do the following in order to make this possible.

1. Download an audio recording application as soon as you are done getting your microphone set up and tested. You will have to sideload the application you want to get in this case. Be sure to refer to the details on this process from earlier in this book to get an idea of how you can do this.

2. Use the appropriate instructions on your program. Note Recorder might be the easiest program to use because it has an extremely straightforward approach to recording notes, for instance.

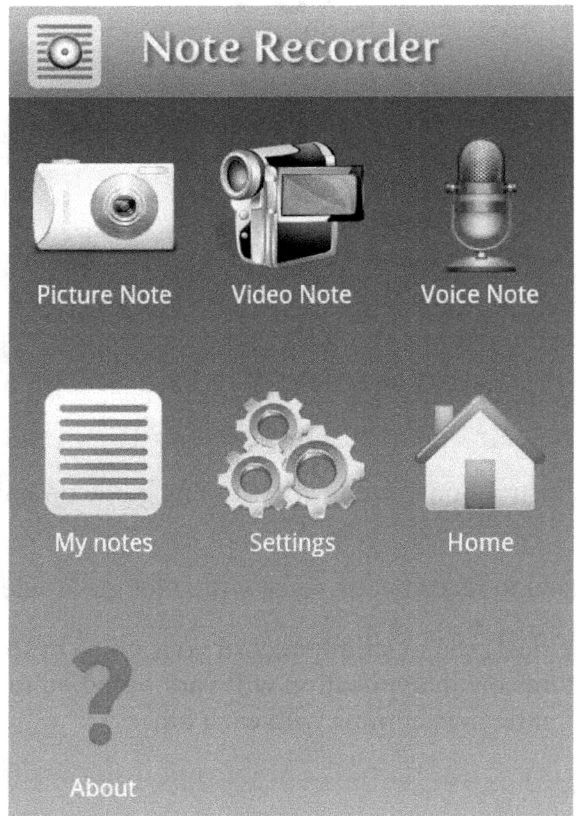

3. Open an appropriate file that you've recorded to test and see if it is working properly. You should be able to open your file up directly with the music player on your reader. Just be sure that the settings on your recording program are set up to where you can actually listen to what you have recorded with an appropriate file format.

141. Microphone Stand

Although you can use a microphone for recording things onto the Kindle Fire, you have to be sure that you use a microphone stand for this case. The problem with not using such a stand is that you will end up dealing with too much audio interference when you are trying to record items onto your reader. This is because you might be too busy holding onto it as you are trying to record a podcast, note or anything else you want to use.

Fortunately, you can find a quality microphone stand in a variety of places. A microphone stand can be used to keep your tablet supported with a simple easel at the bottom and a full extending bar that links your microphone up to your reader. This is all while keeping your reader suspended with a rest.

The steps for setting up your microphone stand will vary based on the specific stand model that you want to se. The following process is a basic series of steps that can be used on most microphone stands.

1. Buy an appropriate microphone stand. It should not cost you more than fifty dollars just to get a stand. The smallest microphone stands (unlike the one in the picture seen above) may cost you less than twenty dollars to get.
2. Use an appropriate clasp for attaching the Kindle Fire onto the stand.
3. Link up your microphone with headphones onto the Kindle Fire.
4. Try and use an appropriate extender to expand the distance between your microphone and your reader. A 3.5mm extended can be used with a 3.5mm jack on both sides of the unit.

This should be used to give you access to a unique way to record things. You might particularly benefit from a stand if you are a podcaster who wants to record episodes of a show that you might have. It makes the process of recording something easier to use.

Chapter 20 – Fun Accessories and Stuff

As you have seen throughout this entire book, the things that you can do with your Kindle Fire or your Kindle Fire HD are all things that add to the functionality of whatever you can get out of your reader.

However, you might be amazed at the different accessories that you can use to add to what goes onto your Kindle Fire. This includes a look at what you might get out of the reader for more than just reading, listening, playing, surfing or whatever it is you already do with it.

142. Special Chargers

The world of Kindle Fire chargers is impressive to see. While you can use a traditional wall charger or a USB charger to power up your Kindle Fire, you could also use a car charger if possible.

1. Plug the appropriate connector into your Kindle Fire. In most cases you will have to plug the USB connector for your reader into a car charging device. You will have to attach the reader to the end of your Kindle Fire and then plug the USB end into the larger bulk end of the charger. However, some chargers may work with just a simple 3.5mm jack and a large power base. The product seen in the picture on top of this tip is an example of what you could be using in this case.

2. Insert the main charging device into your car's electrical outlet. This should be located near the dashboard of your car in most cases.

3. Allow the reader to charge up. You should still have access to the reader's many functions when you use this. Just be aware of what you are getting out of the recharging process because it will take longer for the reader to charge itself up when you are using it while it is plugged into an outlet.

143. Protective Screen

A protective screen can be added to your reader in order to keep the glass screen on your Kindle Fire protected. A screen like this will be clear and can be easily laid out over the tablet without compromising the visibility of your reader.

In addition, this makes it easier for you to keep from having to clean off the reader. While the process used for cleaning off the reader might be easy to use as you might have noticed early on in this guide, a protective screen might still be a better protective material to use when keeping your Kindle Fire screen protected.

1. Take out an appropriate protective screen application. Many companies that sell these screens will sell multiple copies of the same protector because it is so affordable to set up.
2. Lay out the screen protector by using the borders of the protector as a guide. Add this with the top or bottom corners first.
3. Cover the rest of the screen with this protective layer. The entire screen should become flat but still have a small tab to use on one side in order to remove the protective layer as needed.

144. Stylus Pen

A stylus pen is a small material that you can use for tapping the screen with. This can be used to protect your screen from fingerprints while allowing you to have a smaller item with which to interact with your reader with. However, you will have to use a few tips in order to keep this pen working properly.

1. You should be able to use just about any stylus pen that you want to add to your reader. This is because a stylus pen will not have to be plugged into anything on your tablet.
2. Watch for the force you use when taking in a stylus pen. You have to simply use a few tapping motions when using a stylus pen. You don't have to add lots of force onto the screen.
3. Check and see what stylus covers you could use on the tip of your pen. A stylus cover can create a soft buffer between the tip of the pen and the screen.
4. Check on the thickness of the pen. It should be a little slimmer in size than your fingertip. In fact, the thickness can make it look like a real pen but without the use of actual ink.

5. Use an appropriate stand for your stylus pen when you are not using it. This is to keep your pen from laying on a flat surface where it might collect dust and other items.

145. Protective Cover

Adding a protective cover to the body of your Kindle Fire is always a good idea because it covers your reader and adds some insulation to it. It is made to keep your device from being likely to open up and become damaged.

Here are a few tips to use when getting such a protective material like this added to your Kindle Fire.

1. Make sure that the Kindle Fire cover is actually designed to fit in with your specific Kindle Fire model. This includes the seven or 8.9-inch models.
2. Use a cover that features a small design with a few stitch marks to protect the body of the cover so it will not come apart.
3. Check and see if there are any special compartments located around the body of the reader. These compartments can be added to give you something extra.

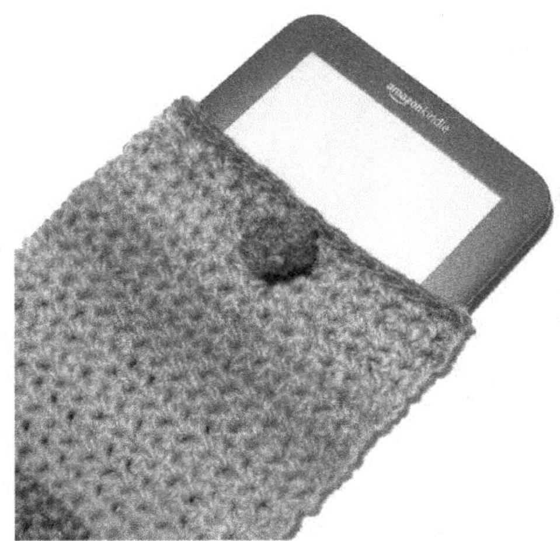

4. Keep the cover steady without having to move the reader out of the cover. While it is true that a thread-based case that you can take the reader in and out of can be attractive, you should be sure that the cover is made to where the reader is easy to store without having to take it out too often. This is to keep the screen protected. However, you can make sure that you use a safe and protective series of fibers on the body of your cover so the screen will not pick up any fibers and clutter up the body of your space.

146. Outside Light

While you can use the light feature on your Kindle Fire to illuminate whatever it is you are reading, this device is going to use more battery power when you keep it illuminated. The energy used to get the internal light working on your Kindle Fire can be a real burden. That's why it is such a good idea to use an outside light source to light up the reader.

You don't have to get a huge light either. You can just get something that will clip itself onto the body of your reader. This will attach itself to the device through a clasp that you can adjust. This process for using it should be easy to operate.

1. Insert an appropriate battery into the outside light. Most of these lights are so small that one single AAA battery may be all you need to get it running.
2. Test the light to see that it can actually start up when you turn it on.

3. Attach the light to a hard edge on the Kindle Fire. The borders around the reader should make it easy for you to attach it without having to obstruct you view of anything. It might be easier if you have a protective cover over the body of the reader as well.

4. Turn on the light and adjust it in the way that you see fit. Most of these readers are designed with special craning necks that let you adjust the light into one of many angles. You can do this to keep the light from creating a glaring effect.

It is true that most of these lights cannot be adjusted in terms of how intense they are. Still, it should not be all that tough for you to create a new light source that will be easy to use without having to use up more battery power on your Kindle Fire than what is needed.

147. Back Seat Attachment

Not every driver can afford to use a DVD player or video screen in the back seat of the vehicle. This makes it tough for you to keep your kids entertained during a long car drive. However, you can fix this problem by adding a back seat attachment feature to your Kindle Fire.

This will allow you to attach your reader to the back of a car headrest. You can use this attachment to create a display that is similar to what you'd find in a high-end luxury vehicle.

1. Find an appropriate attachment that will fit onto the body of your vehicle.

2. Secure the attachment based on the instructions that it comes with.

3. Control your Kindle Fire with the appropriate movements you want to use when starting up a video file for display.

4. Link the Kindle Fire up to the attachment device. This should be supported with a few clasps used to keep the Kindle Fire displayed in a landscape format.

This should provide your car with a new way to entertain people. You can use this to play back videos for your kids to watch or you can use it as a device for carpoolers to use for productivity purposes while traveling en route to work. The functionality of such an attachment makes this all the more beneficial.

148. Adding a Kindle Skin

A Kindle skin is a type of cover that you can place over the physical body of the Kindle Fire. This is designed with a series of art prints, graphics or other unique designs for whatever you might be interested in using. The process of adding such a skin to your Kindle Fire is easy to use.

What makes this all the more appealing is that this can be done with any skin design you want. This process can be used for a pre-made skin or for a skin that is designed with your own customized image. The image has to be supported by the skin manufacturer so you can use a more unique option for display purposes.

1. Buy an appropriate skin that can actually fit your specific model.
2. Attach the skin onto the model by using an appropriate guide on the skin's body. This may include attaching it with one end of the screen first.
3. Use the skin on a flat surface to make it easier for it to be attached onto your reader.
4. Use the outside boundary on the skin to stretch it out to where there will be no air bubbles between the skin and the rest of the reader's body.

149. Removing the Skin

You can also remove the skin quickly with this simple process.

1. Use an appropriate edge of the front part of the Kindle Fire for removing the skin.
2. Peel off the area from one end to the next.
3. Flatten the skin so it can be attached back onto the reader later on if you wish to add it again.

This procedure may be used when replacing the skin with something or when you have to remove the skin for some professional display purpose. Either way, it only takes a few seconds for you to do this.

150. Getting a Custom Skin

The final trick for your Kindle Fire is to create a custom skin that you can use on your Kindle Fire.

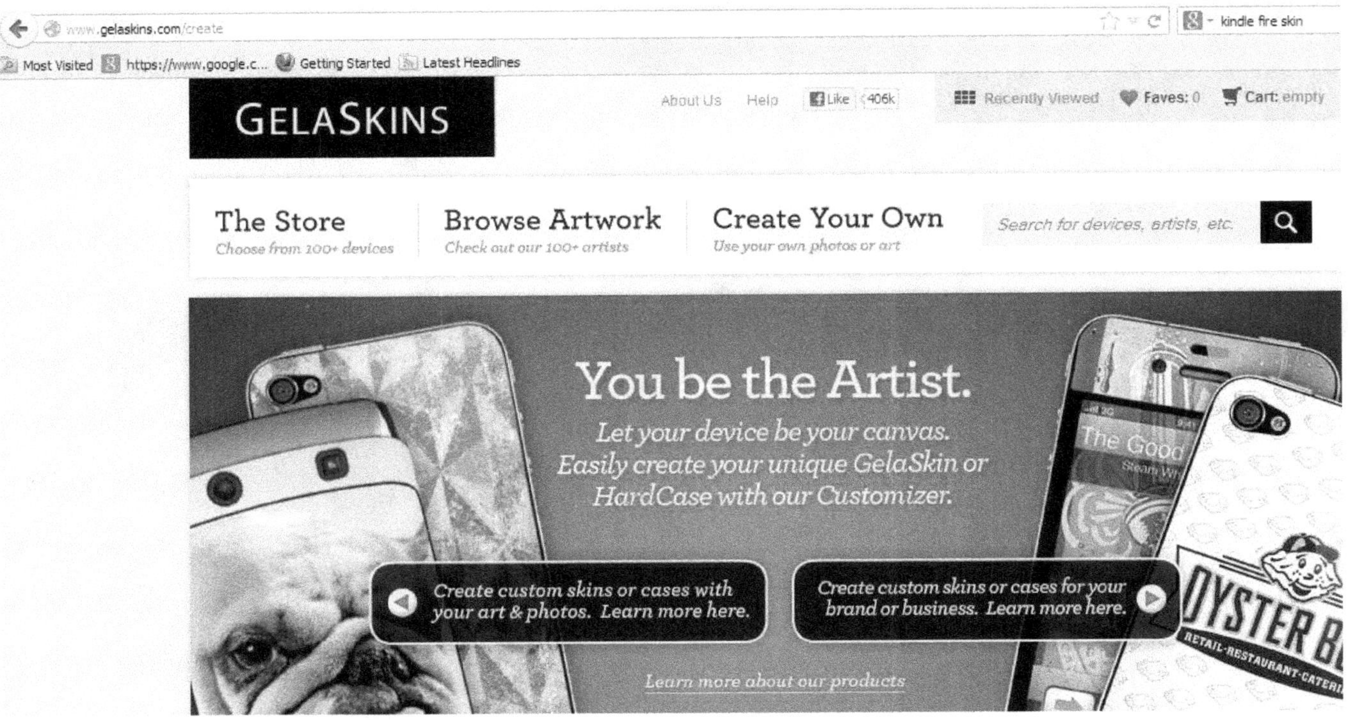

1. Submit an image for a custom skin to a website that can create a new skin for you. The GelaSkins process is the one that will be used in this example to show you how it can be done.
2. Be sure to follow the appropriate standards for what images can be uploaded to the site.
3. Adjust the image through the appropriate editing program used on the website.
4. Check the image preview to see if it will look appropriate for your Kindle Fire.
5. Submit the final request to the company. It should then create a new skin for your reader. It will take longer for this to be delivered due to the special procedure for creating such a skin but it will end up creating a unique look to make it special.

Conclusion

It's amazing to see what you can get out of the Kindle Fire and Kindle Fire HD. You can use the tips and tricks listed in this guide to give you plenty of ideas relating to whatever you want to get out of your reader. You should use these tips to help you out with finding anything of interest for you to use.

The Kindle Fire and Kindle Fire HD are both designed with a number of appealing features that go well beyond the world of portable books. While you can always read books on the Kindle Fire, you can use this to go online, play back media files and even use applications.

The things that you can do are interesting but you should be aware of how you can do so much with whatever model you might have. The Kindle Fire is designed to be useful and suitable for all sorts of special needs that you might have when using it. This includes understanding just what you need to do when you run into different problems while using it.

So, have fun with your Kindle Fire! You will certainly find it to be more fun when you know about everything you can do with it.

www.ingramcontent.com/pod-product-compliance
Lightning Source LLC
Chambersburg PA
CBHW082110070326
40689CB00052B/4472
* 9 7 8 1 4 9 5 2 1 1 0 8 9 *